STURGEON HOOKS OF EURASIA

VIKING FUND PUBLICATIONS IN ANTHROPOLOGY

Number Thirty-Five

STURGEON HOOKS OF EURASIA

by

GÉZA DE ROHAN-CSERMAK

Preface by

ROBERT F. HEIZER

Subscribers edition

distributed through

CURRENT ANTHROPOLOGY

for the

WENNER-GREN FOUNDATION TO ANTHROPOLOGICAL RESEARCH, INCORPORATED

1963

This volume comprises one of a series of publications on research in general anthropology published by the Wenner-Gren Foundation for Anthropological Research, Incorporated, a foundation created and endowed at the instance of Axel L. Wenner-Gren for scientific, educational, and charitable purposes. The reports, numbered consecutively as independent contributions, appear at irregular intervals.

Edited by SOL TAX, University of Chicago

Library of Congress Catalog Card Number 63-9795

Printed in the Netherlands

To the memory of Ottó Herman and János Jankó
two great pioneers of European ethnology

PREFACE

This monograph, as the reader will soon discover, is more than a study limited to hooks for catching sturgeon. It is a study of the sturgeon fishing complex with special emphasis upon catching devices, and is an admirable example of the comparative method applied to an integral set of data in order to reach historical conclusions that are continually checked against old documentary and archeological records. It combines, in short, the synchronic and diachronic approaches.

In central and northern Europe the study of folk cultures constitutes a special kind of ethnography and the present work belongs to that tradition. In general, the idea of peasant cultures as formulated by Robert Redfield, Oscar Lewis and George Foster does not seem to form the broad interpretive base for European studies, most of which are essentially straight reporting like the American Indian ethnographies of forty years ago. The study of European peasant or folk cultures by specialists attached to ethnographical institutes, academies of sciences, and national museums in Hungary, Austria, Finland, Sweden and Poland, for example, involves both the collection of items of material culture (dress, musical instruments, tools, etc.) and the recording of songs, tales, and methods of application of tools and instruments for industrial and economic ends.

In most of Europe a rich historical literature has made available documentary evidence from earlier times that is used to provide time depth to aspects of contemporary folk culture. The archeology of these countries, from the Migration Period on, is very intensively studied, since it provides even greater time depth to the surviving folk cultures. How very useful European folk cultures can be to archeologists is clearly illustrated in J. G. D. Clark's *Prehistoric Europe*. Intense nationalistic feelings have, of course, encouraged the study of modern European peasant cultures and their histories. This is a kind of ethnography that cannot be done in North America north of Mexico, and it is therefore largely unfamiliar to anthropologists in the United States.

The main area investigated in this study is the Danube River, where sturgeon fishery can be shown to have been practiced for the last 3,000 years. Of the Acipenseridae (the sturgeon family), the largest are *Huso huso* of the Black, Azov, and Caspian sea regions, and *Huso dauricus* of the Amur River. The huge size of this fish is illustrated by a Russian catch of one specimen that was

17 meters long and weighed 2,000 kg. (2.2 tons), and of a really giant example that weighed 4,100 kg. (4.5 tons). Sturgeon are easily taken and cannot be described as "game fish" which fight when hooked; rather, they become immobile and completely passive when caught. These great fish ordinarily swim in large numbers near the surface of the water while ascending the rivers for spawning. The reader may be surprised to learn that they are caught with large metal hooks ordinarily set not in the expected fashion—thus: ∪—but exactly opposite—thus: ∩—with a line attached to the hook at the inner bend and tied to a surface float to keep the hook in its reversed position. The sturgeon feeds by lashing food toward its mouth with its tail, and in so doing may be impaled in the tail or breast or mouth by the hook.

The typology of sturgeon hooks is neatly presented here, and one form of hook (Type III) is traced back to Mesolithic forms made of bone. The argument is advanced (pp. 125-126) that the original sturgeon hooks were of the "self-floating" type made of wood and that these go back to a wood-oriented technology ("lignic" culture). The great economic productivity of the seasonal sturgeon fishery is seen (as earlier proposed by Graham Clark) as an important factor in the colonization of the European riverine systems in the Neolithic Age. A peculiar form of Norwegian reindeer antler hook of the Viking period, with a hole below the bend in a flat flange, is identified as a sturgeon hook of the "samolov" type that was set with its point directed downward. The samolov type of hook also occurs among the Gilyak and Orochi in eastern Asia and the form thus may be added to the culture inventory of the ancient north Asiatic Oikoumenê. The samolov type of hook is even in evidence among the prehistoric Point Hope Eskimo population. Thus the investigation of sturgeon hooks adds to our knowledge of the prehistoric culture connections between the Eastern and Western hemispheres. The broadest generalization that G. de Rohan-Csermak makes (pp. 127-28) is that Eurasiatic fishery began on the inland riverine waters and has only comparatively recently spread out to the coasts and open sea.

In his consideration of the types of hooks and their distributions in space and time, the author encounters the problem of deciding whether he is dealing with instances of convergence or historical connection over very great distances when he finds hooks that are closely similar in form. This is a common type of problem in distributional analyses, and the author uses both typological and functional criteria in reaching a decision.

The excellent use of linguistic evidence for determining sources of hook types or techniques of sturgeon fishing is of considerable methodological interest, as is the exact and detailed historical tracing of events connected with the diffusion of this form of fishery. Archeologists quite obviously have a necessarily oversimplified view of the diffusion of material forms, and documented examples such as sturgeon hooks, while perhaps of no immediate concern to a prehistorian, nevertheless give him a sobering example of the nonlogical, even capricious, events that may be involved in the culture process we call diffusion. Thus, for example, the "Iron Gate," where the Danube emerges into its broad lower course from the Carpathian mountains, marks a pronounced boundary dividing the occurrence of certain fishing implements and techniques. Before 1837 the Iron Gate was closed to ship traffic, and this barrier seems to have worked effectively against the diffusion of sturgeon fishing gear. Political events in 1837, leading to the regulation of the Iron Gate, brought about regular ship traffic, and with this came the upstream dissemination of fishing techniques.

Beyond all this, I believe this monograph represents the kind of useful and stimulating study of material culture that has unfortunately gone out of vogue in American ethnology. Such investigations are contributions to the grand aim of anthropology, which is the complete knowledge of the facts and total understanding of the processes involved in the cultural history of man. I see this work on sturgeon hooks as an excellent piece of scholarly investigation of methodological interest, and one that reaffirms the importance to anthropology of studies of material culture.

This study, further, represents a new addition to the limited number of classic anthropological studies of fishing listed in the accompanying bibliography

Robert F. Heizer.

BIBLIOGRAPHY

BATES, H. W.
   1917. "Ancient Egyptian Fishing." ("Harvard African Studies," 1: 199-271.) Cambridge, Mass.

FINDEISEN, H.
   1929. "Die Fischerie im Leben der 'Altsibirischen' Volkerstämme," *Anthropos*, 60: 1-72.

HAMMEL, E. A. and YNEZ D. HAASE
   1962. "A Survey of Peruvian Fishing Communities." ("U. of Calif. Anthropological Records," 21: 211-30.) Berkeley, Calif.

KROEBER, A. L. and S. A. BARRETT
   1960. "Fishing Among the Indians of Northwestern California." ("U. of Calif. Anthropological Records," Vol. 21, No. 1.) Berkeley, Calif.

RODRIGUEZ SANTAMARIA, B.
   1923. *Diccionario de artes de pesca de España y sus posesiones*. Madrid.

ROSTLUND, E.
   1952. "Freshwater Fish and Fishing in Native North America." ("U. of Calif. Pubs. in Geography," Vol. 9.") Berkeley, Calif.

SANEZ REQUART, A.
   1791-95. *Diccionario historico de las artes de la pesca nacional*. 4 vols. Madrid.

FOREWORD

Investigation into European folk life must be brought to an abstract level to be made ready for a comprehensive synthesis. This is necessary if European ethnology is to deserve the name of "science" in the modern, philosophical sense of the term. Abstractness of the investigational methods and results—which automatically creates the necessity of a synthetic survey—is, by the way, the fundamental requirement of all scientific disciplines.

While those descriptive monographs which are published in great numbers and are rooted in the traditions of the classic European "ethnography" are surely indispensable for the construction of a truly European ethnology, their integration cannot be achieved without a process of abstraction. Yet a very great number of details will still have to be investigated with the comparative method before European ethnology can hope to obtain such results regarding the cultural evolution of the Continent and the interethnic contacts of its peoples as have, for instance, been reached in the field of linguistics.

Of course, research work cannot stop at the ethnic or geographical boundaries of the European continent, because ethnological phenomena cannot be truly understood unless the cultures of the Asiatic and even more distant peoples are also taken into account.

It was with such considerations in mind that I wrote the present monograph. I consider myself a disciple of Ottó Herman and János Jankó—those two great pioneers of European ethnology—as regards horizontal analysis (the comparison of recent phenomena) and vertical analysis (the exploration of historical traces). These make up the "complex method" (complex in the widest sense of the word) of these two prominent investigators, both of whom passed away nearly a half-century ago, and should serve as a model for all students of European ethnology. First of all, it is to the researches of these two investigators that I owe gratitude for the inception of this work.

I am much indebted to Professor H. V. Vallois, Director of the Musée de l'Homme, Paris, who was kind enough to make possible and to direct my researches. I would also like to express my appreciation to Professor Sol Tax for his help toward publication of this book. Further, thanks are due my fellow workers, who gave ready and valuable assistance.

In the text, bibliography and footnotes the rules observed are those prescribed by the "International System for the Transliteration of Cyrillic Characters" (*International Standard Organisation—Recommandation R 9*, Genève, 1954) for the transliteration of words written in the Russian alphabet. This system is employed also by UNESCO (cf. Francis Kent [director of the Library of the UNESCO], "Progrès internationaux dans le domaine de la translittéra-

XI

tion," *Bulletin de l'Unesco à l'intention des bibliothèques*, X, Nos. 5–6, 139–141. Paris, 1956).

The drawings in the text are by András Csikós-Tóth of Budapest and Roger Humbert of Paris. The photographs for the plates are by József Franciscy of Budapest and René Pasquino of Paris. My grateful acknowledgement is extended to them for their excellent work.

Géza de Rohan-Csermak

TABLE OF CONTENTS

STURGEON HOOKS OF EURASIA

CHAPTER I

THE STURGEON

I. ITS HISTORICAL AND ECONOMIC SIGNIFICANCE

ACIPENSERIDAE OCCUPY a special position in both natural history and ethnography. Quite a number of ichthyological treatises discuss them at length, while ethnographers and ethnologists attribute great importance to sturgeon in the folk life of those areas where this fish abounds. It will not be superfluous, then, by way of introduction, to outline the factors that have secured such a prominent place for the sturgeon family.

Acipenseridae owe their distinguished position to their economic value. The flesh of the sturgeon, a widely popular foodstuff, contains no bones, only cartilage, and can be stored well. Preserved by various techniques, sturgeon flesh has always formed an important item in world trade. Whether under the name of τάριχος, as it was called by the fishermen of antiquity who caught the sturgeon in the Borysthenes River and in the Meotis (the Dnieper River and the Sea of Azov, respectively, in our day), or under the name of балык, as it is called nowadays by the fishermen of southern Russia, it has never been absent from world markets. Equally important is the roe of this fish; caviar, prepared from it, has been known as a relish since the Middle Ages in many countries. The sturgeon air bladder has been used for the preparation of isinglass since antiquity, and the skin also forms a commercially valuable item.

As a foodstuff, the sturgeon has always been a very expensive and favorite delicacy. When the first shiploads of sturgeon flesh arrived at the port of Athens, a single amphora from it was more expensive than a whole "hecatomba," that is, a hundred sheep and a bull. Sturgeon was one of the most appreciated table delicacies in ancient Rome. Adorned with garlands of flowers, the dish was served with the accompaniment of songs and flutes at the banquets of the rich. The sturgeon was supplied from the Danube for the tables of the emperor and the aristocracy of Byzantium.

Sturgeon was no less important in other parts of Europe. According to an ancient law of Jutland, it and other fish of similar size belonged to the king, the same as did the objects saved from shipwrecks. A law promulgated by Edward II of England announced that sturgeon caught along the seashore was to be the property of the King and that such fish caught in the Thames were to belong to the Lord Mayor of London. The *droit d'esturgeon*—the ownership of all sturgeon caught in any river from the Seine to the Rhone—

I

constituted a privilege of the aristocracy and the high clergy in medieval France, which privilege was conferred on them by the sovereign. Alfonso II of Aragon, when making fishery free for the fishermen along the Ebro in 1165, reserved for himself the right to have sturgeon caught in that river delivered to the royal household.

Those places in the rivers which were suitable for the fishing of the so-called "great sturgeon" (hausen, beluga, or huso as it will be called in the following discussion) formed the subject of special royal grants in Russia and Hungary. Only those ethnic groups enjoying the special benevolence of the Tsar, such as the Cossacks of the Dnieper (Zaporozhian Cossacks), the Don, and the Ural, were allowed to participate in the traditional annual great sturgeon fishing along the big rivers of southern Russia. Huso, as an item of the export trade, was second in rank only to cattle in Hungary from the Middle Ages up to the eighteenth century. Hungarian huso was sold in Poland, Austria, Moravia, Germany, and even France.

The commercial importance of the sturgeon was the same in the Far East too. Only the emperor had the right to consume the flesh of the Chinese sturgeon *(Acipenser sinensis)* in China, for which reason its Chinese name means "im-perial fish". The situation must have been the same in Japan, where the indigenous variety *(A. mikadoi)* is known as "imperial sturgeon" among biologists.

It is, however, not only their character as a gastronomic delicacy that determines the economic significance of Acipenseridae; it owes much more to the facts that fishes of that family are large, that they appear in vast numbers during the seasonal run, and that they are comparatively easy to catch. *Acipenser huso*, the giant of the family, is known to be the largest fresh-water fish in the world. Specimens with a length of 9 meters and a weight of 1,400 kilograms were caught in the middle (Hungarian) stretch of the Danube only a few centuries ago. A record from the eighteenth century mentions a specimen caught in Russia that was 17 meters long and weighed 2,000 kilograms.

This enormous size is also expressed by the Persian name of the huso, "fil-mahi," which, literally translated, means "elephant-fish." The other sturgeon species, although smaller, still are among the largest fish. For example, the common sturgeon *(Acipenser sturio)*, which is the most widely distributed, sometimes attains the length of 6 meters.

Usually twice a year, in spring and in autumn, the great sturgeon ascend the rivers from the sea and migrate in dense crowds towards the higher stretches. Apart from these seasonal runs, the midwinter, too, is a propitious time for sturgeon fishing, when the fish hiding in the holes of the river bed are stirred up and caught. These occasions are veritable feasts for the fishermen, and sturgeon is so abundant that it would be senseless for them to concern themselves with any other kind of fish at these times. Catches are sometimes so large that a few days' work often results in more fish than are caught at all other times during the whole year.

This being the case, we have to accept G. Clark's statement that the annual run of sturgeon was a factor in the colonization of the riparian regions during the Neolithic Age.

Let us add that, in our opinion, the direction of the seasonal run of the sturgeon was one of the most important factors during the Völkerwanderung (Great Migration) that made peoples decide to take a route that led them from east to west across the southern Russian plain. This, above all, applied to the nomadic stock-raising Hungarians, who were the most important people to traverse this region between the fifth and ninth centuries. The ancient Hungarians consistently followed the lower stretches of those rivers which flow into the Caspian and the Black Sea until they arrived at the Carpathians in 895 and there terminated their migration in the Carpathian Basin, where the waters also abounded in sturgeon.[1] We know from contemporary Arabian and Byzantine sources that the nomad Magyars moved to the river valleys in winter and that these valleys were the scenes of large-scale sturgeon fishing. Search for adequate pastures was the men's chief occupation during the other seasons. This pastoral and fishing mode of life has been characteristic of the nomadic peoples in this area up to quite recent times. It should be emphasized that this nomadic form of life should be sharply distinguished from other forms of nomadism, especially from nomadism in southwestern and central Asia, though hath forms are frequently treated by ethnologists under the collective term, "steppe nomadism." It is, above all, the seasonal fishery that forms a sharp dividing line between the pastoral civilization of the peoples of the Völkerwanderung in the Ural-Danube area and the steppe civilization of all other Eurasian stock-raising peoples.

A good analogy is offered by another important Eurasian fishing area. Salmon fishing played quite as important a role in northern Europe as did sturgeon fishing in the life of the steppe peoples between the Ural and Danube rivers. Kustaa Vilkuna was concerned with this phenomenon and arrived at the same conclusions in respect to salmon fishing as are presented in respect to sturgeon fishing[2] in this monograph.

1. Since the ancient Magyars (Hungarians) are repeatedly mentioned in the monograph, it will be expedient to adduce certain historical data concerning them.

The Magyar people, of Finno-Ugrian origin, separated themselves from the Ugrian branch of the Finno-Ugrians, at about 1000 B.C., to start an independent life on the European side of the Ural Mountains. Around the time of Christ's birth the ethnic group of the ancient Magyars crossed the Urals into Asia, where—abandoning their forest-dwelling, fishing, hunting, and gathering manner of life—they adopted a primitive form of equestrian-nomadic mode of life. The migration of the Turkish peoples, coming from the east, reached the Magyars in this region in the fifth century. Joining the Bulgaro-Turkish peoples in quest of a new home, the Magyars moved to the region bounded by the lower stretch of the Don, the Black Sea, the Caucasus, the Caspian Sea, and the Volga. Here they became familiar with up-to-date forms of stock-breeding and agriculture, while their ancient fishing-hunting culture was enriched with new elements. About the year 800, the Magyars marched to the area lying east of the Don River. Being attacked once more from the east in 889, they moved westward and occupied the area between the Don and the delta of the Danube. Renewed attacks forced them to leave this area too and move, in 895, to the Carpathian Basin, their final home.

2. Cf. Vilkuna (1954 and 1956).

The stock of sturgeon in the rivers, which was immensely rich in prehistoric and historic times, is now on the wane, and the size of the fish caught by the fishermen is becoming demonstrably smaller and smaller. In the Middle Ages large shoals of sturgeon used to ascend the Thames, Seine, Ebro, Po, and the upper stretches of the Danube, while nowadays large-scale fishing of sturgeon is confined to the Balkan portion of the Danube and the rivers of the southern Russian plain. Sturgeon fishery is still so important in the Soviet Union that its results constitute a significant separate item in the national income. This used to be the case also in England, France, Spain, Hungary, and presumably in northern Italy, although, today, the capture of a large sturgeon is reported by the press of these countries as headline news.

Ethnologically, sturgeon fishing may be divided into separate elements. Of special interest is the monumental apparatus of sturgeon fishery, namely the weir across the river, a widespread contraption in central and southeastern Europe during historical times. Several ethnographers have studied this sturgeon-catching device, and it formed the subject of a lively debate among Hungarian investigators some years ago.[3]

Problems connected with sturgeon hooks are likewise of fundamental importance. Descriptions and references contained in historical sources are in this respect unfortunately less numerous and accurate than those concerning weirs. A comparative study of their morphological changes and their distribution may, however, likewise be attempted on a Eurasian scale, and it is possible that the results of archeology may prove useful in this field.

A monographic treatment of sturgeon hooks provides opportunity to elucidate a number of ethnographic problems and to throw light on the origin of fishhooks in general. The range of this monograph extends beyond the problems concerning a single given fishing gear serving the capture of a single given kind of fish and is intended to illuminate a very important point of contact between the respective material cultures of different Eurasian peoples, a contact that points to even more remote cultural relationships.

2. GEOGRAPHICAL DISTRIBUTION OF ACIPENSERIDAE IN EURASIA

Acipenseridae are distributed all over Europe and northern, central, and eastern Asia and occur also in North America (Fig. 1).

The largest in size among the European and Near Eastern members of the family is the great sturgeon *(Huso huso*, formerly *Acipenser huso)*, to be found in the Black Sea, the Sea of Azov, and the Caspian Sea, and also in the rivers drained by them (Pl. I). It appeared in historical times (and still appears, though rarely) in certain rivers of the Adriatic Sea, for example, in the Po

---

3. The polemic concerning huso weirs, started by Károly Gaál, was fought out in *Ethnographia*, the gazette of the Hungarian Ethnographical Society. An opposite view was then announced by Péter Morvay, following which Márta Belényesy defined her attitude in the matter. (See Bibliography.)

River. Another variety, the Amur sturgeon *(Huso dauricus)*, occurs in the Amur River, in its tributaries, and around its estuary.

The most widely distributed western European member of the family is the common sturgeon *(Acipenser sturio)*, which is encountered anywhere between Europe's northernmost regions and the Black Sea. It occurs oc-

FIGURE I.—Distribution of Acipenseridae in Eurasia. (After Berg and Magnin, completed.) ||||||||, distribution of the European and Far Eastern great sturgeon (huso).

casionally even in Iceland. *Acipenser naccari* is the sturgeon inhabiting the Adriatic Sea. Though more indigenous in the eastern parts of Europe, the stellate sturgeon *(A. stellatus)* can also occasionally be found in the Adriatic.

The Black, Azov, and Caspian seas, together with the vast area pervaded by the rivers drained by these waters, should be regarded as the original and true home of the sturgeon. Indigenous in these waters are, as has been noted, the huso, the common sturgeon, and the stellate sturgeon. Likewise in this region is encountered a very important variety, the Russian sturgeon *(A. güldenstädti)*, which lives only in rivers. Also found here are the bastard sturgeon *(A. nudiventris,* formerly *A. schypa)* and, one of the smallest members of the family, the sterlet *(A. ruthenus)*. The bastard sturgeon also inhabits Lake Aral and its rivers, while the sterlet lives in the rivers of the Arctic Ocean, from those of the White Sea to the Yenisei. A characteristic variety found in the rivers emptying into Arctic Ocean is the Siberian sturgeon *(A. baeri)*; it is quite common in the rivers traversing the area between the Ob and the Kolyma and around their estuaries, but occurs sometimes even east of the Ob River.

The Amu-Daria and Sir-Daria rivers, both emptying into Lake Aral, are the habitat of the smallest sturgeon (the flat-nosed *Pseudoscaphirhynchus kaufmanni, Ps. hermanni* and *Ps. fedtschenkoi*).

In the Far East, the Amur River, its estuary, and its tributaries are very rich in sturgeon. It is here that (apart from the afore mentioned *Huso dauricus*) we find the most important variety, namely the *Acipenser schrenki*. The green sturgeon *(A. medirostris)* inhabits the coastal waters of the northern Pacific Ocean on both the Asiatic and the American sides.

The imperial sturgeon *(A. mikadoi)*, which inhabits the fresh waters of Japan and Korea has already been mentioned; another kind, *A. kikuchii*, occurs also in these waters. The Chinese sturgeon *(A. sinensis)* is widespread in Chinese rivers, while the Yangtze Kiang is the home of the yellow sturgeon *(A. dabrianus)*, and *A. kiangsinensis* is found in the Si-Kiang. Since the Chinese names of *Huso dauricus* and *Acipenser schrenki* are also mentioned in Russian ichthyological sources, it can be assumed that these varieties inhabit Chinese waters as well.

CHAPTER II

THE CHARACTER OF STURGEON HOOKS

I. A BIOLOGICAL FEATURE OF STURGEON AS A SHAPING FACTOR OF HOOKS

EUROPEAN FISHING TOOLS include a kind of hook that is different from, and much larger than, any other hook used in river fishery and whose manipulation is similar to that of no other fishing gear. It is the sturgeon hook. The subject of this monograph.

Ordinary hooks catch fish by being placed in the water with or without bait; the animal, mistaking it for food, snaps it up and, according to the construction of the hook and the nature of the suspected prey, the hook is then either swallowed or gets stuck in the mouth of the fish, which is thus caught and remains suspended by the line attached to the hook. When fishing by means of hooks is spoken of, this technique of catching is always meant.

The situation is fundamentally different in the case of sturgeon. Members of the family Acipenseridae get stuck by plunging their tail into the hook. Petrović observes that the great sturgeon is always caught behind its breast fins—"under the armpit," as Serbian fishermen say—or at its tail, with which it is incessantly lashing out during its rapid swimming and fighting and which, therefore is most exposed to the danger of being caught by the pointed hooks.[1] Nyiry was told by fishermen who worked in the neighborhood of Szentes on the Tisza River that the hook usually penetrated the orifice of the alimentary canal in sterlets.[2]

There are various theories to explain this peculiar phenomenon. The most popular explanation is that sturgeons, "frolicsome" creatures, like to "play" with objects crossing their path and that it is by this "playfulness" that they come to grief.[3] Much more reasonable seems to be another theory, according to which the observed behavior is due to the sturgeon's manner of getting hold of foodstuffs, a technique evolued by these fish because of their physical constitution. It should be noted that the mouth of Acipenseridae lies deeply beneath the nose and that they drive foodstuffs to the oral aperture by a lash of the tail.[4] This hypothesis appears to be the more satisfactory, since sturgeon

1. Петровић (1941), p. 78.
2. Nyíri (1946–47), p. 286.
3. Heckel (1863), p. 212; Rómer (1866), XXI, 1; Сабанеев (1892), II, 558; Szurmay (1926), p.45; Khin (1928), p. 50; Manninen (1932), p. 273; Arnaud (1936), p. 33; Schrenck (1881–95), III, 521.
4. Ecsedi (1933), p. 173; Nyíri (1946-47), p. 286.

is not a common fish of prey but the omnivorous descendant of an ancient form.[5] That the sturgeon often gets stuck by the mouth is in no way contradictory to the theory that it throws its food to its mouth with a jerk of the tail. What happens in such a case is that the fish strikes the harmless side of the hook that it does not pierce the flesh until it has been snapped up with the mouth.

This congenital feature of Acipenseridae has necessitated the development of specially shaped hooks and a special technique for their manipulation. In order the hook should not get caught by the mouth but should pierce the body of the fish, it was necessary to transform or adapt the hooks used for catching other kinds of fish. This adaptation always remained moderate and never occurred in disregard of those ancient hook types which were rooted in the respective traditions of the temporally and spatially diverging popular civilizations. This is an instance of "survival," so well known to folklorists, and may be called a "formal relict." It will be discussed more in detail in the course of the monograph.

Another natural feature of Acipenseridae that favors the use of hooks is that when the hook pierces its skin, the sturgeon—after moving for a short time—becomes immobile and lies quietly in the water, although its skin is so strong that not even heavy jerks could tear it open. Although the hooks are usually arranged in a densely packed row, the wound inflicted on the body of the sturgeon consists of only one or more minute punctures because of the quiescence of the animal after it has been caught.[6] The behavior of Acipenseridae after having taken the hook is so passive that, according to Arnaud, their resistance is less than that of algae.[7] Only in the knowledge of such passivity can one understand that, giants as they are, neither stronger nor larger hooks are needed to catch them. The dimensions of sturgeon hooks, though exceeding those of other hooks, are slight in proportion to the bulk of the catch.

It has been mentioned that all hooks required for the fishing of sturgeon of any variety were made after a more or less similar pattern. Yet we have records concerning the history of only the hook used for the huso, the largest fish of the Danube. The span-long huso hook was the only kind used by Danubian sturgeon fishers at the time of Otto Herman's investigations. Less

5. "Voracious, they pursue small fry, but sometimes swallow even wild ducks and also floating bulrush, roots and pieces of wood . . ." (Szinnyei [1863], p. 131). This is confirmed almost verbatim by Sabaneev who reports that duck and pieces of wood were found in the animal. He writes that it seizes the food with the mouth but lifts it from the bottom with the tail (Сабанеев [1892], II, 521 and 525). F. Rómer remarks in his notes that fishermen of Apatin found large pieces of stone and wood in the stomach of the great sturgeon (Rómer [1866], XXI, 1). The great huso of the Caspian Sea is, according to Russian investigators, a typical animal of prey. The young of the species consume small crabs, small fish, and algae. They adopt subsequently a fish diet, devouring herring and other fish. Therefore, the sojourn of the huso largely depends on the places where such fish happen to assemble. Sometimes large specimens of the huso devour even young seals (Танасийчук [1951], pp. 15-16).

6. Herman (1887), I, 217; Сабанеев (1892), II, 558; Blanchère (1885), p. 297.

7. Arnaud (1936), p. 33.

bulky varieties of sturgeon also ascend the Danube at the time of the seasonal migrations, and it is noteworthy that, up to quite recent times, the Danubian fishermen have not invented or used any special device for the fishing of this smaller fry, not even a reduced copy of the large huso hook. Sterlet hooks have been in use only a short time but have now become very popular. These are exactly like huso hooks, only much smaller, as is natural in view of the fact that, as regards bodily constitution and biological properties, sterlet is a diminutive replica of sturgeon.

2. THE NAMES OF THE STURGEON HOOK IN EUROPE

Although adopted at different times, the Danubian huso hook and sterlet hook—both of which undoubtedly show the characteristics of a common type— have a common name at some places along the river.

The Russian language, on the other hand, has separate words for huso, sturgeon, and sterlet hooks. The word in most general use is самолов, which means "automatically catching"[8] and designates, nowadays, not merely hooks provided with floats but pendent baitless huso hooks as well. All other types of hooks are known as перемёт. Less general but more accurate expressions to signify sturgeon hooks are балберочная снасть or шашковая снасть meaning "floated hooks" (i.e., hooks provided with floats). Further details in this respect will be given below.[9]

The word *carmac* is used by the Balkan peoples living on the banks of the Danube to distinguish huso and sterlet hooks from all other kinds of hooks. The word *carmac* is, according to Gmelin, of Tataric origin; it is still used in the estuary of the Volga, but there it has a different meaning, for originally it served to designate a platformed lifting hook used by the fishermen in the Astrakhan area in the eighteenth century for catching salmon during the winter season.[10]

Almost certainly the word *carmac* (and as will be seen, also the tool that it denotes) was brought to the Danube by those Lipovan fishermen who had settled at the delta of the river. The word кармак, as understood by them, meant the entire fishing gear.[11] Although adopted in unchanged form by the Rumanian fishermen, *carmac* there means the old huso hook only.[12] The same applies to the Bulgarians, who use the word кармац likewise for the hook itself.[13] The word такуми inherited from the Turks, is employed by Serbian fishermen to indicate a whole row of huso hooks.[14]

8. Definition of the term "самолов" is to be found in nearly all Russian works on fishing. For a more detailed interpretation see Варпаховский (1898), p. 34.

9. See sec. 1 of Chap. IV.

10. Gmelin (1774–84), II, 215.

11. Вовк (1899), p. 40.

12. Antipa (1916) and Ghelase (1951), *passim*.

13. Андреев (1922), p. 125.

14. Петровић (1941), p. 75.

The hooks serve to catch different varieties of sturgeon, and those hooks with which this monograph is concerned will be called "hooks of the samolov type" or simply *samolovs*. This word has already been used by Jankó[15] and Manninen,[16] so it may be regarded as one accepted in international literature.

The single but decisive criterion of hooks of the samolov type is that they capture fish by getting stuck, in their body. Besides this principal criterion, hooks of this type reveal other characteristics of morphology, structure, and manipulation that serve to distinguish varieties of the samolov.

3. THE MORPHOLOGY OF HOOKS OF THE SAMOLOV TYPE

The crook of hooks of the samolov type is elongated, straight, and tapering. It forms an acute angle with the shank of the hook, the crook and shank are rarely parallel, and the crook is never bent toward the shank. The crook is sharply pointed. The length of the hook varies according to that of the fish to be caught: huso hooks are from 12 to 19 cm. long (and most frequently 16–17 cm.), while shorter hooks are used for the smaller varieties. Sterlet hooks have the smallest size, with a length of about 5 cm. (Fig. 2).

4. THE STRUCTURE OF HOOKS OF THE SAMOLOV TYPE

A unique structural feature of samolovs is that the barb of the hook does not serve the same purpose as that of other types, which is to prevent the crook from slipping out of the body once the point has entered. The crook does not penetrate beyond the skin in the case of Acipenseridae; since these fish remain quiet after being caught, there is no necessity for barbs of large size. Only the modern, industrially manufactured sturgeon hooks are provided with barbs that prevent backslip. The barb of forged sturgeon hooks is just a coign, which has the function of preventing the float line from slipping off the crook. The barb of the hooks of the samolov type, therefore, does not correspond to what is known as *Widerhaken* in German literature; it is only a protruding peg, often merely a slight thickening of the crook.

5. MANIPULATION OF HOOKS OF THE SAMOLOV TYPE

Hooks of this type are usually unbaited,[17] while nearly all other types everywhere are provided with a natural or artificial bait.[18]

15. Jankó (1900), pp. 521–22 and *passim*.

16. Manninen (1934), p. 65.

17. Herman distinguishes it from all other types of hook in the following words: "devoid of bait" (Herman [1887], I, 353). Some of the recent huso hooks are provided with bait, as is mentioned in connection with Russian hooks.

18. It is quite surprising that, sometimes perhaps rather unnecessarily, the use of bait is mostly connected with the notion of hooks. Thomazi was the first to note that baitless hooks might suffice in places where fish are very abundant or voracious. In tropical seas, abounding with

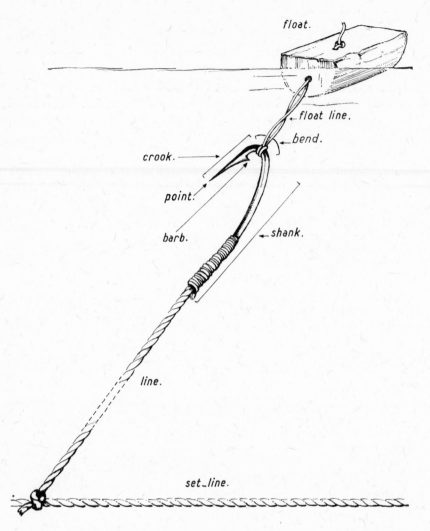

float.

←float line.

←bend.

crook.→

point.

barb.

←shank.

line.

set_line.

FIGURE 2.—The most general form of sturgeon hook of the samolov type and its terminology as used in the text.

animal life, it is enough to cast the hook into the water; it will be attacked by the fish as if it were some exquisite delicacy. "The natives provide, as a rule, their hooks with bait nevertheless, and there is hardly anyone among them who does not know what kind of bait to employ for the fish he wants to catch" (Thomazi [1947], p. 99). Sirelius dissents from this view. It is, according to him, a general principle among primitive peoples to use unbaited hooks; he adds that the use of artificial baits, employed in lieu of real ones, is nevertheless frequent (Sirelius [1934], p. 100).

All these data justify the statement that the use of natural or artifical bait is probably universal. Yet we must not include those angling devices which are regarded by Sirelius as belonging to the category of *active* fishhooks as distinguished from *passive* tools like the samolov. What is meant by the word "active" will be clear if we think of the *bagov* used in South Russia or the unbaited hooks that, suspended in a densely packed row, are employed in eastern Asia for a veritable raking of the water. Such tools could safely be classified under the head of "searching tools," a term coined by Herman and applied by him to nets only. To provide bait with such active hooks would, of course, make no sense.

Another peculiarity of the samolovs is that they are afloat. The terms "floating hook" or "swimming hook" are frequently used to indicate the samolov type of hook. While most of the hooks used in river fishery lie at the bottom of the water, samolovs are kept a little below its surface by means of floats.

There are various modes of attaching the float to the hook, and these will be discussed in detail in a later chapter. Only a brief outline of the classic form of attachment is necessary here. This form is unique and cannot be seen in connection with any other kind of hook; it consists in fastening the float line to the bend of the hook, that is, to the point where crook and shank meet. This mode of attachment alters the usual basic position of the hook. While the bend of the hook points downward and the point of the crook is directed upward in all other types, these respective positions of bend and point are reversed in the case of samolovs. By pointing upward, the hook occupies the most suitable position for utilizing the tail-lashing movements of the sturgeon.

CHAPTER III

CENTRAL AND SOUTHEASTERN EUROPEAN
(DANUBIAN) HOOKS

THE HUSO, THIS giant of the Danube, the largest fresh-water fish in the world, has inhabited the rivers of the Danube Basin since prehistoric times. Huso is undoubtedly the most important item in the fishery of the Danubian peoples. Since the flesh of the huso provided excellent and savory food, could be sold at a low price, and the fish itself was comparatively easy to catch, it is no wonder that all other kinds of fishery were neglected when innumerable shoals of the great sturgeon began to ascend the Danube and its larger tributaries.[1] Huso had reigned supreme in Danubian fishery from time immemorial, continued to do so until the eighteenth century between Pozsony (now Bratislava) and the Iron Gate, and is still doing so between the Iron Gate and the Black Sea. The great sturgeon played a less conspicuous role on the upper stretch of the Danube (between Pozsony and Bavaria) during the Middle Ages.

An approximate picture of Danubian huso fishing in historical times can be reconstructed from the geographical descriptions of classic authors[2] and also from scattered data contained in German works on natural history[3] from the twelfth and thirteenth centuries. It is no exaggeration to say that the vast shoals of huso ascending the Danube practically offered themselves to the fishermen.[4] What we want to know is how and by means of which tools the huso was caught. Consistent with the scope of this monograph, an attempt

1. Although both the number and the size of sturgeon are on the wane in Russia, hauls made there still convey a good idea of the abundance of Acipenseridae in the lower Danube before the eighteenth century and in the middle Danube prior to the middle of the sixteenth century. Reports of journeys on the Volga and the Ob make it probable that practically nothing but sturgeon could also have played a significant role in Danubian fishery.

Moynet, writing in the middle of the last century, states that fishermen of the Volga hold small fish in contempt; small fry, salted and dried, are sent to the interior of the empire, while sturgeon and huso enjoy high esteem (Moynet [1867], p. 84). A report on fishery on and around the Ob River written in the second half of the eighteenth century by Pallas holds the same view. Sturgeon was so abundant there that smaller fish were simply thrown away (Pallas [1771–76], III, 84).

2. It will suffice to refer to reports of Herodotos, Strabon, Cassiodorus, Plinius, and Aelianus on huso fishing.

3. Such as Thomas Cantimpratensis, Konrad von Megenberg, Vicentius Bellovacensis, and Albertus Magnus.

4. Chap. III, sec. 7, will show numerically that, while Acipenseridae are mostly represented by stellate sturgeon and Russian sturgeon in the waters of Russia, huso is the reigning fish in the Danube. That hauls were so rich in the middle Danube was also due to the fact that mostly great

will be made to answer the following question: Since when and in what parts of the Danube has huso been captured by means of hooks?

As will be seen, many findings have only local validity and cannot be applied to Danubian fishery in general. It seems that the Iron Gate and the "cataracts" (the torrential part where the Danube breaks through the Carpathian range) formed a dividing line in the spread of certain fishing tools, including huso hooks. Up to the middle of the nineteenth century, fishing customs along the Balkan stretch of the river were fundamentally different from those existing along the middle portion of the Danube (Fig. 3).

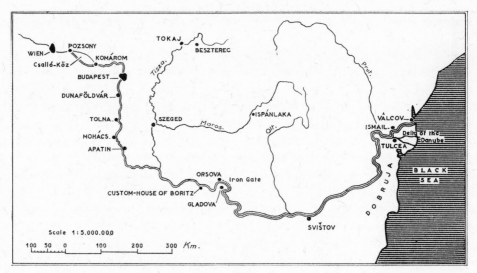

FIGURE 3.—Map of the Danube Basin with names of places occurring in the text. ▬▬▬, middle Danube, between Pozsony (now Bratislava) and the Iron Gate, called also "Hungarian Danube," since it formed part of Hungary for a millennium, until 1919. ▬▬▬, lower Danube or Balkan Danube, the "Ister" of antiquity, between the Iron Gate and the delta.

This difference was, in the main, due to the fact that the unregulated Iron Gate constituted a formidable obstacle, which hampered the movement of fishermen very seriously. This natural barrier prevented the free diffusion of cultural elements. It is known in ethnology that great bodies of water are especially suitable for the transmission of culture and for the cultural equalization of remote territories; such cultural transmission long remained impossible in this case.

specimens used to arrive there during the seasonal sturgeon migrations. That always huge specimens are mentioned in historical records should not be understood to mean that smaller fish were disregarded. Numerous data adduced by Sabaneev confirm his assumption that the largest specimens of huso managed to ascend farthest upstream (Сабанеев [1892], II, 517.) It seems that up to the end of the first millennium of our era, shoals of huso ascended as far as Bavaria, while Pozsony had become their farthest boundary by the time of the Árpád dynasty. It was at this time that the middle Danube became the abode of the largest spawning sturgeon.

It would actually be tempting to assemble in a separate essay all those historical data that refer to the abundance of huso in the Danube.

The regulation of the Iron Gate, accomplished by István Széchenyi in 1837, brought a radical change in this respect. Before the regulation, the occasional passage of a wooden vessel through the cataracts of the Iron Gate was a sensational event, but after 1837 undisturbed shipping became a matter of course. At about this time the first regular steamer service was established. Since then, any new fishing tool to appear on the Balkan Danube was brought by the boatmen upstream and this spread over the middle stretches in a few decades.

I. A BRONZE HUSO HOOK FROM THE EARLY IRON AGE

Among the prehistoric archeological finds, only one hook has been encountered that must surely have been used as a huso hook (Pl. II, No. 1).

The hook in question was unearthed in Transylvania, at the boundary of the counties Alsófehér and Küküllő, near Ispánlaka (Rumanian: Şpălnaca), 6 kilometers southeast of Marosujvár. The whole excavated material of bronze weighed about 800 kilograms and was first described by G. Téglás and later, in more detail, by Zs. Reiner. The latter described several objects in the find but made no mention of any hook. Almost half a century went by before the first publication of this ethnographically important piece of the find appeared. The material excavated at Ispánlaka was transferred to the Archaeological Museum of Bucharest and was described by Hortensia Dumitrescu after its arrival there. After having analyzed most of the pieces of the material very carefully, she remarked casually: "Besides these tools the collection contains less significant pieces as well. Let us mention a hook constructed of four-edged small bars . . ."[5] How little attention she was paying to this piece, which is unique of its kind, is shown by the fact that no dimensions were given in the description of the hook, although exact dimensions were given for all other objects. However, compared to the objects lying beside it, the hook evidently is 14 centimeters long. Dumitrescu in this connection refers to a bronze hook described by Hampel; this is quite wrong, since Hampel's tool is merely an ordinary sheatfish hook.

The shape of the bronze huso hook found at Ispánlaka does not differ from those of recent sturgeon hooks, and the ending of its shank shows that its made of attachment was likewise similar. It is unbarbed. The shank is four-edged, that is, its cross section is rectangular. The hook was presumably not made by bending a straight bar but must have been cast. The bend is directed not toward the flat side of the bar but toward its edge—in the direction of the diagonal of the square-shaped cross section. This construction is quite different from that seen in modern hooks and seems to have served for strengthening the material (bronze, which is much softer than iron).

The hook under review belongs to the early Iron Age, the time of transition between the Hallstatt periods A and B, which, according to archeology, was

5. Dumitrescu (1935–36), p. 214; illustration, p. 219, Fig. 14, No. 5.

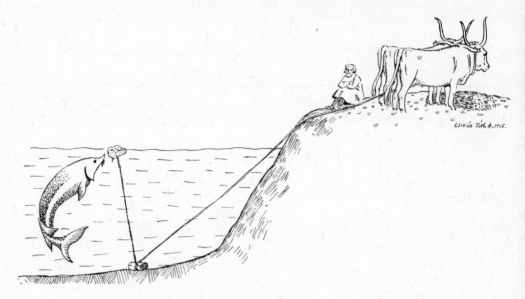

FIGURE 4.—Fishing by means of the huso hook with the aid of animals. Lower Danube. (Reconstructed after the description of Aelianus.)

not later than about 900 B.C. We must bear in mind that fishing tools can be used a long time, so bronze hooks may have survived for one or even two centuries after their first appearance in the Danubian wilderness. From this it follows that bronze hooks were probably employed down to 800 or 700 B.C.

The hook was found next to the Maros River and not far from the Olt River. Since both rivers lead to the Balkan stretch of the Danube, it can be assumed that the bronze material of Ispánlaka was brought from or was intended to be conveyed to the Danube by its prehistoric owner, probably an itinerant peddler. Huso, by the way, used to ascend both rivers even as late as the middle of the last century[6] and may have occurred in them in much greater numbers at the time that this hook was still in actual use. It is, however, more probable that such hooks were in use at the richer fishing places of the Balkan Danube—if the comparative degree of this adjective is justified in view of the immeasurable abundance of fish at those times.

Two conclusions may be drawn regarding the huso hook of Ispánlaka: it has now been proved (1) that Danubian man of the Hallstatt civilization caught sturgeon with hooks and (2) that the form of these hooks has remained essentially unchanged during three millennia.

2. HUSO HOOKS AS USED IN ANTIQUITY

Aelianus (born in the second half of the second century A.D. and still alive in 222), having observed huso fishing in the Balkan Danube, described it in the following terms (Fig. 4):

6. Huso was indigenous to the Maros and Olt rivers even in comparatively recent times, i.e., in the first half of the last century (Heckel [1863], p. 212).

Ἀνὴρ Ἰστριανὸς γένος, τὴν τέχνην ἁλιεύς, τῆς τοῦ Ἴστρου ὄχθης πλησίον ἐλαύνει βοῶν ζεῦγος, οὔ τι που δεόμενος ἀροῦν οὗτος· ὥσπερ γάρ φησιν ὁ λόγος, μηδὲν εἶναι βοῒ κοινὸν καὶ δελφῖνι, οὕτω τοι φιλία χερσὶν ἁλιέων καὶ ἀρότρῳ πόθεν ἂν γένοιτο; εἰ οὖν οἱ καὶ ἵππων παρείη ζεῦγος, τοῖς ἵπποις χρῆται. καὶ τὸν μὲν ζυγὸν ὁ ἀνὴρ φέρει κατὰ τῶν ὤμων, ἔρχεται δὲ ἔνθα οἱ δοκεῖ καλῶς ἔχειν ἑαυτὸν καθίσαι καὶ ἐν καλῷ τῆς ἄγρας εἶναι πεπίστευκε. τῆς οὖν μηρίνθου στερεᾶς οὔσης καὶ ἄγαν ἑλκτικῆς τὴν μὲν ἀρχὴν ἐξῆψε μέσου τοῦ ζυγοῦ, ἄδην δὲ τροφῆς παρατίθησιν ἢ τοῖς βουσὶν ἢ τοῖς ἵπποις, οἳ δὲ ἐμπίπλανται. καὶ ἐκεῖνος τῇ μηρίνθῳ κατὰ θάτερα προσῆψεν ἄγκιστρον ἰσχυρὸν καὶ μέντοι καὶ τεθηγμένον δεινῶς, περιπείρας δὲ ἄρα αὐτῷ πνεύμονα ταύρου, μεθῆκε τροφὴν Ἰστριανῷ σιλούρῳ καὶ μάλα γε ἡδίστην, ὑπὲρ τοῦ συνδέοντος τὸ ἄγκιστρον λίνου ἐξάψας τὸν ἀρκοῦντα μόλιβον, οἷον ἐς τὴν ἕλξιν εἶναι ἔρμα αὐτόν. ὁ τοίνυν ἰχθὺς ὁπόταν αἴσθηται τῆς ταυρείου βορᾶς παραχρῆμα κατὰ τὴν ἄγραν ὁρμᾷ, εἶτα ὧν ἱμείρει τούτοις ἐντυχὼν ἀθρόως· καὶ περιχανὼν ἄδην καὶ ἀταμιεύτως τὴν ἐμπεσοῦσάν οἱ κακὴν δαῖτα ἐς ἑαυτὸν σπᾷ. εἶτα ὑφ' ἡδονῆς ἑλιττόμενος ὅδε ὁ γάστρις ἑαυτὸν διαλέληθε τῷ προειρημένῳ περιπαρεὶς ἀγκίστρῳ, καὶ ἀποδρᾶναι τὸ ἐμπεσὸν κακὸν διφῶν τὴν μήρινθον ὡς ἔχει δυνάμεως ὑποταράττει τε καὶ κινεῖ. συνίησιν οὖν ὁ θηρατὴς καὶ ἡδονῆς ὑπερεμπίπλαται, εἶτα τῆς ἕδρας ἀνέθορε, καὶ μεθῆκεν ἑαυτὸν ποταμίων τε ἔργων καὶ κυνηγεσίων ἐνύδρων, ὥσπερ δὲ ἐν δράματι ὑποκριτὴς ἀμείψας προσωπεῖον ὃ δὲ τὼ βόε ἐλαύνει ἢ τὼ ἵππω, ἀλκὴ δὲ ἄρα καὶ ἡ τοῦ κήτους καὶ ἡ τῶν ὑποζυγίων ἀντίπαλός ἐστιν. ὁ μὲν γὰρ θὴρ ὁ τοῦ Ἴστρου τρόφιμος ἕλκει κάτω ὅσον ποτὲ ἄρα τῆς ἐν αὐτῷ ῥώμης ἔχει, τὸ μέντοι ζεῦγος τὸ ἀνθέλκον ἐκτείνει τὴν μήρινθον. ἀλλά οἱ πλέον οὐδὲ ἕν· τῆς γοῦν ἐπ' ἀμφοῖν ἕλξεως ὁ ἰχθὺς ἥττᾶται, καὶ ἀπειπὼν ἕλκεται κατὰ τῆς ᾐόνος.[7]

An Istrian, a fisherman by profession, is driving a pair of oxen on the bank of the Ister. He does not need them for ploughing. They say that ox and dolphin have nothing in common: how could the fisherman use his arms for handling the plough? If, however, he has a team of horses, he uses horses. The man carries the yoke on his shoulders and goes to a place where he thinks he will find a good seat and can make a good haul. There he fastens the end of a strong rope, one well suited for drawing, to the middle of the yoke. He provides ample fodder for the oxen or the horses, and they eat their fill. To the other and of the rope, he attaches a strong and sharply pointed hook, onto which he spikes the lung of a bull, so offering a favorite delicacy of the large Istrian fish, after fastening a piece of lead to the rope from which the hook is suspended sufficiently heavy to prevent it from being carried away from the bottom. As soon as the fish becomes aware of the bull's meat, it darts to seize it. Then, having reached what it was looking for, all at once, with its open and gluttonous throat, it swallows the dangerous food. Then it splashes about happily, and so the reveller impales itself unawares onto the aforesaid hook. And while it tries to escape from the evil thing thus picked up, it agitates thirstily and shakes the rope with great force. Seeing this, the fisherman is filled with joy; he jumps up from his seat, abandons his preoccupation with the river and his aquatic hunt. And, like an actor in a play changing his mask, he drives his pair of oxen or horses. The force of the draught-animal is pitched against the strength of the aquatic animal. The creature of the Ister pulls with all its strength toward the depth, while the yoke is pulled in the opposite direction, and the rope becomes taut. But this does not help the fish: at any rate, it is the loser in the double pull and, exhausted, it is dragged ashore.

7. Aelianus (1864–66), lib. XIV, cap. 25.

Aelianus, dealing once more with huso fishing on the lower Danube in his next chapter, now writes explicitly of ἀντακαῖος, that is, huso. From this chapter only that passage which describes fishing with the huso hook is quoted.

Χειμῶνος δὲ λήγοντος καὶ ὑπαρχομένου ἦρος καὶ ἐλευθέρου τοῦ Ἴστρου ῥέοντος μισεῖ τὴν ἀργίαν καὶ ἀναπλεύσας ἐμφορεῖται τοῦ κατὰ τὸ ὕδωρ ἀφροῦ· πολὺς δὲ οὗτός ἐστι μορμύροντος τοῦ ῥεύματος καὶ ὠθουμένου σφοδρότατα. ἐνταῦθά τοι καὶ ἁλίσκεται ῥᾳδίως, ἐλλοχώντων αὐτὸν τῶν ἁλιέων καὶ τὸ ἄγκιστρον ἐς τὸν ἀφρὸν καθιέντων σὺν τῇ ὁρμιᾷ. καὶ τὸ μὲν κρύπτεται ὑπὸ τῇ λευκότητι, καὶ ἡ αἴγλη τοῦ χαλκοῦ εὐσύνοπτός οἱ οὐκ ἔστι, καὶ διὰ ταῦτά τοι περιχανὼν καὶ λάβρως σπῶν τοῦ προειρημένου σιτίου καταπίνει τὸν δόλον, καὶ ἀπόλωλεν ἐντεῦθεν ὅθεν τὰ πρῶτα ἐτρέφετο.[8]

At the end of winter and the beginning of spring, when the Ister is streaming uncurbed, it [the huso] gets to hate inactivity, shoots up to the surface and gets covered with the foam of the water which arises in great masses as the river roars and boils in violent tumult. It is easily caught here. The fishermen lie in wait for it and let the hook sink with the rope into the foam. The white spume hides the hook so that not even the sparkling of the bronze remains visible; hence, as the fish opens its jaws and takes a heavy draught of the aforesaid food, it swallows the bait and meets its death from the very thing that before sustained it.

These highly instructive passages require explanation. The fish caught in the described manner is called σίλουρος by Aelianus in his twenty-fifth chapter. The word has a double sense: it may mean any large river fish or it may mean sheatfish, the largest inhabitant of Hellenic rivers. These two meanings are accepted by the best Greek dictionaries. It is, however, evident from Scaliger's description that this word was frequently used to signify sturgeon. This author lived at the beginning of the sixteenth century and discussed at length the error of certain authors who identified *silurus* with *sturio*.[9]

The problem is solved by a synonym contained in a later part of the text; where Aelianus applied another word to the same kind of fish.[10] He uses the word κῆτος, which means a large sea fish or a cetacean, in general, and a dolphin, in particular. Since there are no cateceans in the Danube, the word could have applied to the great sturgeon, which is the only kind to ascend the river from the Black Sea. In the course of further investigations description by Herodotos was found explicitly likening the huso (ἀντακαῖος) to the whale (κῆτος).[11]

A few recent data will add to the completeness of the argument. Even

8. Aelianus (1864–66), lib. XIV, cap. 26.

9. Scaliger (1557), exerc. CCXVIII, cap. 3, pp. 288–89.

10. K. Marót, professor of classical philology in Budapest University, called attention to this solution.

11. Herodotos writes of the Βορυσθένης the following: κήτεά τε μεγάλα ἀνάκανθα, τὰ ἀντακαίους καλέουσι, that is, "it offers also large boneless cetaceans (dolphins), called 'antakaios' [= huso]" (Herodotos [1909], lib. IV, cap. 53, p. 344).

fishermen of our own day are wont to liken the huso to the dolphin. Белуга means "dolphin" on the shores of the White Sea and "huso" in southern Russia.[12] This identity was the cause of much worry to Gmelin, Pallas, and other explorers of the eighteenth century. It is an interesting fact that the word "beluga" or "belouga" is used by the fishermen of Brittany to define either a dolphin or another cetacean, a porpoise (in French, "dauphin" and "marsouin," respectively). Again, fishermen of the Danube Delta describe the great sturgeon as "white dolphin."[13]

While these considerations leave no doubt that "large fish" must have referred to huso in the text of Aelianus, the manner of fishing as he outlined it furnishes additional argument in favor of the allegation that the "large fish" could be nothing but great sturgeon:

a) To emphasize that the hook was sharply pointed would have been super-fluous in the case of a sheatfish hook. Only the unusually sharp point of the huso hook could induce the classic author to lay special stress on this feature. Archeological finds make it clear that sheatfish hooks of antiquity were not more sharply pointed than are the hooks with which this fish is caught nowa-days.[14]

b) At first sight, the expression "lung of a fattened bull" seems to indicate a simple bait. It must, however, be remembered that neither the lung of cattle nor that of any other animal is used as bait anywhere along the Danube. Why did the fisherman of Aelianus not use the kind of bait still regarded as most successful by the Danubian fishermen who want to entice sheatfish, for example, various kinds of maggots or living small fish, which, writhing, attract these large animals of prey? An immobile piece of flesh is not the right bait to entice sheatfish. Why was it necessary to fasten a piece of fat cattle lung to the hook?

Animal lung has a property that makes it different from all other animal organs: it remains afloat.[15] The author found it necessary to emphasize that the lung had been taken from a fat animal because a fatty lung is capable of withstanding longer the water's decomposing and dissolving action. The bait is thus also a float in this case, which keeps the hook afloat by pulling it toward the surface of the water. Sheatfish do not snap at bait swimming on the surface, while sturgeon do—as a matter of fact they like nothing better, as has been proved in numberless instances. As to the piece of lead fastened to the rope, it must have served as a simple weight to prevent the hook from being swept away by the current.

12 Данилевский (1862), pp. 83–84, 143, 144, 148, and *passim.*

13. Arnaud (1936), p. 26.

14. An iron sheatfish hook was found near Tinosul, on the bank of the Prahova River, a tributary of the lower Danube. It is of approximately the same age as that reported by Aelianus and is similar to modern sheatfish hooks. Its point forms an obtuse angle, and its size (82 mm.) is like that of recent forged middle Danubian sheatfish hooks (R. Vulpe and E. Vulpe [1924], p. 218, Fig. 47, No. 19; p. 219, Fig. 48, No. 5).

15. Cooks can tell that, while being boiled, it will remain on the surface for a long time.

c) The manner in which the catch is described as having been hauled ashore also argues for huso and against sheatfish. It is known that sheatfish, with which the Danube abounded in those times, sometimes reached enormous dimensions, and we can therefore well believe that animal force was needed to haul a sheatfish of 100–150 kilograms to the beach. Acceptable as this supposition appears at first sight, we must ask whether sheatfish are suitable for this manner of handling. Experience argues against it, and no recent instance is known of sheatfish having been caught in this way. Publications on European fishing methods do not seem to contain descriptions in which sheatfish were hauled in by animal force; neither are these reports on such an arrangement of the hook line as would rigidly fix the hook and pitch it against the efforts of the sheatfish. Fishermen along European rivers are wont to tire out sheatfish. When the fish is caught, they pay out the line, that is, the animal is played on the line; after having been relaxed, the line is carefully drawn back; when the fish begins to jerk on the line very heavily, it is let out once more, and so on until the animal is worn out and can easily be hauled ashore or lifted into the boat. (Hauling must have been the more usual procedure during the use of easily capsizing monoxyles.) It should be noted that only in rare instances does the hook catch the mouth of the fish by its bony portion, which can resist heavy jerks. Again, no line exists that would be thin enough to be attached to the hook and, at the same time, strong enough to withstand the pull of a large sheatfish. Nor is there evidence of sheatfish hooks whose line is tied to a rigid tree; it is always attached to some flexible piece of wood, which the fishermen plant in the soil of the bank as a precaution against the danger of its being carried away; if this happens, the stake emerges from the water, thus indicating the whereabouts of the prey. All these facts prove that sheatfish are not simply hauled to the shore in the manner described by Aelianus and that the scene be depicted must have been one of huso fishing.

J. Grossinger, a famous Hungarian Jesuit natural scientist of the eighteenth century, offended in his national pride, protested against the etymology of Adelung (a similarly famous contemporary linguist) for the word *huso*: "They derive the Latin *huso* and the German *Hausen* from the Turkish *uzon*, which means long. Why not from the Hungarian words *úszó* ["swimming, floating"] or *húzó* ["pulling"], considering that the great sturgeon has to be hauled so laboriously and is hauled from the river Volga with the aid of two oxen?"[16]

The employment of animals in huso fishery was quite usual along the Volga even as late as a century ago. Šul'c, in describing the manner of fishing under the ice of the Volga by means of samolovs, mentions that huso caught by the row of serial hooks are hauled to the ice with the aid of horses.[17] Large speci-

---

16. Grossinger (1794), p. 64. His remark is the more noteworthy since he was the first to make a comparison between Danubian and Russian fishery. It is regrettable that he omitted reference to the source of his information.

17. Шульц (1861), p. 42.

mens of the great sturgeon are nowadays pulled to the land by means of a reeling device or pulley.[18]

S. Takáts, relying on the evidence of documents, reports that when the fishermen of Komárom (Hungarian Danube) happened to catch several great sturgeon in their net, they beached them with the aid of horses.[19]

No further arguments seem necessary to prove that the words σίλουρος and κῆτος in the text of Aelianus signify huso and that therefore chapter 25 of his book furnishes information about one of the methods employed in antiquity for catching the great sturgeon in the lower portion of the Danube.

The passage quoted from chapter 26 explicitly mentions huso (ἀντακαῖος). The authenticity of this source is strikingly brought out by the author's description of how the great sturgeon hides in its nest in winter and how it dashes forth in spring; this behavior is in complete agreement with present knowledge of the fish. The yellowish and foaming scum, floating in heaps and drifting on the water's surface, is a characteristic feature of the swelling Danube. The bronze hook thrown into it sinks to the bottom unless held up by a float.

Somewhat misleading is the remark of our classic author that the sparkling of the bronze is hidden by the foam. No foam is necessary for this trick, since metal loses its luster in use in any case. It is, on the other hand, proved by numberless recent data that hooks are polished and so kept lustrous by fishermen just for the purpose of attracting the great sturgeon. The description makes it clear in any case that an unbaited hook was used in the given instance.

Apart from other details, what can safely be concluded from the two passages of Aelianus is that huso was caught by means of floating hooks in the lower Danube as long ago as the first to third centuries A.D. and that single hooks, not rows of serially suspended hooks, were employed.

3. THE APPEARANCE OF HUSO HOOKS IN MODERN TIMES

Numerous records, exist concerning huso fishing as it was practiced from the eleventh century in the middle stretch of the Danube (between Pozsony and Orsova). Documents found in various archives refer mostly to the weir (Hungarian, *cége*; Serbian, гарде; Rumanian, *gărduit*) as the chief tool of sturgeon fishery. Sturgeon nets are also frequently mentioned, especially in connection with statutes regarding them. That no hooks are mentioned in any of the early documents is explained by Grossinger at the end of the eighteenth century: "No great or common sturgeon is caught with hooks; if the fishermen succeed in cornering the fish, they transfix it with poleaxes or harpoons."[20]

Grossinger's work was, prior to O. Herman, the fundamental ethnographic

18. Сабанеев (1892), II, 527.
19. Takáts (1897), p. 439.
20. Grossinger (1794), p. 86.

source concerning fishery in the Carpathian Basin. The authenticity of his data is substantiated by his detailed descriptions, his comprehensive knowledge of Hungarian fishery, and his references to the information obtained from simple fishermen.

In addition, a document exists in which I. Mátyus, a doctor in Transylvania in the second half of the eighteenth century, describes how sturgeon are caught in Hungary by means of nets and refers to a different usage along the Po River in Italy, where hooks are used for a similar purpose.[21] Although not said explicitly, it is obvious that—to the author's knowledge—sturgeon hooks were unknown among Hungarian fishermen, since otherwise Mátyus would not have mentioned them as a peculiarity of Italian fishery.

Apart from these two sources, which can be considered direct proofs that huso hooks were not in use along the middle portion of the Danube, there are numerous indirect proofs, such as the innumerable descriptions of huso fishing from the eighteenth century, none of which contains any mention of hooks.

It is therefore safe to conclude that huso hooks were unknown in the middle Danube during the eighteenth century. The absence of references to hooks in the documents is also proof that sturgeon fishery was not practiced by means of hooks in this portion of the Danube at any time between the eleventh and eighteenth centuries. This statement is further substantiated by S. Takáts, who, in his description of huso fishing at Komárom in the eighteenth century, mentions three methods of catching great sturgeon—weirs, harpoons, and nets,[22]—without making any reference to hooks.

4. ANCHOR-SHAPED HUSO HOOKS

Relying chiefly on excavated tools and other material, Kolčin, a Soviet archeologist, presents a description of smithery in Russia in the pre-Mongolian era. His book, published a few years ago, mentions hooksmiths удник as a special branch of the handicraft. These artisans manufactured not merely hooks but all kinds of fishing tools. Among them was a hook with three forks (Fig. 5); it was 39 centimeters long, with a distance of about 22 centimeters between two adjacent points. Both these dimensions, and also the sharpness of the points and the outward bend of the crooks, were quite similar to recent huso hooks.[23] Kolčin dates his hook from the eleventh to the twelfth century.[24] It was unearthed at the former Knažaja Gora, near the Dnieper, south of Kiev,[25] in the vicinity of a river that was inhabited in those times by the giant sturgeon in even larger numbers than in our day.[26] Therefore the anchor-

21. K. Mátyus (1787), pp. 338, 337.

22. Takáts (1897), p. 438.

23. Колчин (1953/A), p. 100.

24. *Ibid.*, p. 254.

25. *Ibid.*, p. 16.

26. Reference to the vast numbers of huso in the Dnieper (Βορυσθένης) and to the fact that they were preserved by salt had already been made by Herodotos (Herodotos [1909], lib. IV, cap. 53). His description and the information given by other antique authors convey a vivid

shaped fossil hook found by the Soviet archeologist must surely have served the purpose of catching Acipenseridae, huso in particular, if one is to judge from the size of the hook.

Data show that Galician fishermen could be found around the Danube Delta as far back as the middle of the twelfth century.[27] They must have arrived there via the Prut or the Dniester River. It is safe to assume also that fishery, as practiced on the Dnieper, which traverses the more eastern regions of the Ukraine, was directly or indirectly connected with the fishing practices of the Danube Delta. The proximity of the mouths of the Dnieper and the

FIGURE 5.—Anchor-shaped tridentate iron hook for huso fishing, from the eleventh to the twelfth century. Knjažaja Gora, Dnieper. (After Kolčin.)

Danube supports this assumption. It is therefore not impossible that anchor-shaped huso hooks were also in use on the lower Danube at the time from which the excavated anchor-shaped huso hook is dated.

J. Libay prepared an attractive colored map of the whole length of the Danube in 1788 and adorned its margin with drawings of various scenes. Two of the drawings illustrate Danubian huso fishing at four different places. The first picture shows fishermen at Komárom and Buda as they are hauling the

picture of the great extent of fishery that must have served the highly developed fish-processing industry. Köhler writes of the Borysthenes as the most significant river—at least the second after the Nile—of the world in those times (Koehler [1832], p. 357). His still unexcelled pertinent historical paper and Ebert's summary work on the culture of southern Russia in antique times contain ample information about huso and sturgeon fishery in the northern regions of the Pontus and also about the role played by the exportation of salted fish (τάριχος) in antiquity.

27. Bobk (1899), p. 33.

great sturgeon ashore in their nets. The second represents huso fishing in the region of the Iron Gate, near the Custom-House of Boritz, east of Galambóc, at the first cataract (near Gladova, now Kladovo). Worthy of special note for our purposes is the second picture (Pl. II, No. 2; Fig. 6) [28] on which there is the following comment:

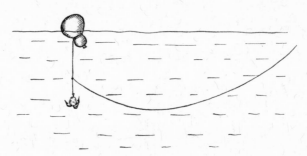

FIGURE 6.—Setup of the anchor-shaped huso hook in the eighteenth century. Region of Iron Gate, Danube. (Reconstructed from the picture and explanatory text on the margin of J. Libay's manuscript Danube map.) For Libay's drawing see Plate II, No. 2.

1. Wird ein Körbus [Kürbis] genommen, an die hänget das Lueder mit dem Ancker und wann der Haussen das Ketter [Köder] schlinget, so bekommet er den Angel mit an den ist ein Strick, so bald der Körbus zücket, so hänget der Fisch an Angel.

Bey No. 2. ist ein Irweg gemacht zu end hänget das Ketter, wie gemöldt ist oben. An No. 1. wird der Fisch an das Land gezogen. No. 2. wird mit Beillen an Irweg erschlagen, allhier wird der Haussen gesalzen verkaufft, und weit verwürdt. [29]

They take a pumpkin from which the carrion with the anchor is suspended; when the sturgeon swallows the bait, it catches also the hook suspended from the rope, so the pumpkin is wrenched and the fish is caught.

In picture No. 2. a labyrinth is made, to the end of which the bait is attached as told above. In picture No. 1. the fish is hauled ashore, and in picture No. 2. it is knocked dead with felling axes the hausen is sold there salted, and is then disposed of farther away.

Libay's description reveals a surprising similarity to that of Aelianus. Although the hook is explicitly mentioned here, it is a solitary floating hook and not a row of serially suspended hooks. The bait consists of carrion, although it is no longer the lung of fat cattle but an undefined piece of flesh. Therefore, a pumpkin, that is, a special float, is needed to keep the hook swimming. The pumpkin is evidently a hollow cucurbit *(Cucurbita lagenaria)*, which is still used by fishermen all over the Danubian river system.

This manner of fishing is reminiscent of the technique that was used in huso fishing as late as World War I, when fishermen around the delta of the Danube caught the great sturgeon by means of anchor-shaped single hooks hanging from boats: "This is customary in the lower portion of the Danube,

28. Picture No. 5 at the foot of Libay's map.
29. This text is immediately above the picture.

especially in the three arms of the estuary; this manner of fishing is particularly popular at Sulina and Tulcea, since these people are the most skilled fishermen of the lower Danube," wrote an amateur angler over forty years ago. We learn from his colorful report that the fishermen of the estuary throw two strong 100-meter long flaxen ropes into the water from their boats and that a three-pronged, anchor-shaped huso hook is suspended from each of the ropes. A piece of offensive-smelling, pinkish, salted beef (perhaps precisely a cattle lung) is so fastened to the hooks that it covers the whole iron. The hook line is let into the water by means of a hand reel.

Portions of the line 5–6 meters long have to be drawn back into the boat by sudden jerks until only about 10 meters of it remain in the water. The line, so drawn back from the water, is reeled up and then paid out once more and jerked back again. The huso does not snatch at objects swimming with, but only objects moving against, the current; it follows them at first and snaps them up only when the supposed prey tends to move toward the surface"—so says the report. Huso, thus caught by the hook, gives a tug to the rope and then allows itself resignedly to be hauled ashore.[30]

The hook of the lower Danube, as described by Libay and Faltay, shows the shape of an anchor, and is similar to that described by O. Herman (Fig. 7)[31]

FIGURE 7.—Anchor-shaped chained huso hook. Straits of Kazan. Region of Iron Gate, Danube. (After Herman.)

30. Faltay (1915), pp. 107–8. To be noted also in this instance is the likeness to Aelianus' description. The reports of Libay and Faltay are further arguments for the equivalence of the words σίλουρος and "great sturgeon."

31. Herman (1887), I, 369. His drawing of the hook is to be found in Fig. 249.

under the name of "chained huso hook". Herman remarks that it is chiefly
used in the area of the Straits of Kazan (i.e., the narrowest section of the Iron
Gate, where the current is swiftest), and this is exactly the area where Libay,
too, observed this kind of hook. In Herman's time this hook was no longer
used singly but was used serially, in rows, which obstructed the passage of
fish swimming upstream (Fig. 8). The description of the hook is continued as

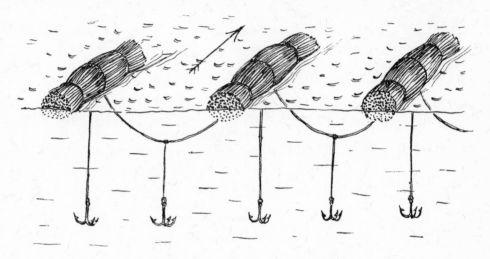

FIGURE 8.—The use of serially suspended anchor-shaped chained huso hooks. Region of Iron
Gate, Danube. (Reconstructed from the description by Heckel and Herman and Alt's two
lithographs.)

follows: "The *horogderék* [principal chain] is the strongest kind of boat-chain
from which several *cserkelánc* [side chains] are suspended at suitable intervals....
The *deréklánc* [principal chain] has a length of 160–200 meters, and each gang
of fishermen owns several such chains." Although Herman's figure represents
a tridentate hook, he observes in the explanatory text that the anchor (macs-
kahorog, "cathook") usually has only two points and that three-pronged
hooks are less frequent.[32] The Budapest Ethnographical Museum owns three
such tridentate hooks collected by Herman (Pl. III, Nos. 1 and 2; Pl. IV,
No. 1)[33], and there is one such hook in the possession of the Budapest Agricultural Museum (Pl. IV, No. 2), but all of them are chainless. None seems to
be identical with that shown in the figure.

There is evidence of the existence of chained hooks in the Carpathian Basin
as far back as the sixteenth century. I. Szamota quotes a passage from a
document of 1587 that was in the archives of the Hungarian family of Nádasdy:
"Horogra walo chykot Keth meritö zakot Lanczos horgoth" ("A loach as
bait for the hook, two dipping bags, a chained hook").[34] The fact that loach

32. Herman (1887), I, 368.
33. Inventory numbers of the Budapest Ethnographical Museum: 32.984, 32.982, and 32.983.
34. Szamota (1894), p. 493.

as a bait and two "dipping bags" are mentioned in the text makes it evident that the hook must have been a fishing tool. The word "chained" points to a large hook, presumably used for sheatfish. Unfortunately, the document gives no geographical definition, but the bulk of the Nádasdy estates was situated in the vicinity of Lake Fertö, the Hanság, and in the region of the Rábaköz (all in West Hungary); the family also possessed less significant landed property near Lake Balaton and in the regions adjacent to the Muraköz and the upper portion of the Save River. Moreover, they had the right of usufruct at Mártély on the banks of the Tisza River.[35] Since the investigations of K. Lukács[36] show that loach fishing had great significance in the region Fertö-Hanság-Rábaköz, it is reasonable to conclude from the reference to loach as bait that this is the area we are looking for. Szamota's laconic information therefore allows at least the conclusion that chained hooks were also used in the sixteenth century for sheatfish in the lakes and marshes of the northwestern corner of Transdanubia.[37]

The description gives no information as to how the "cathooks" described by Herman were set up. The artistic lithographs of J. Alt from the second decade of the nineteenth century contain, however, two instructive illustrations of huso fishing in the lower Danube. The first represents the sturgeon weir at Wirbicza (now Vrbica, 10 km. east of Gladowa) near the straits of Kazan (Pl. V, No. 1).[38] The water has to pass through three rows of serially suspended hooks set up before the weir. The floats consist of large bundles of twigs, enlarged versions of the mat floats still in use on Lake Balaton. These giant floats could have served only for the maintenance of chained hooks. We find the same arrangement of the sturgeon weir in the vicinity of Tufeschty (now Svištov) (Pl. V, No. 2).[39] It is likewise by three rows of hooks that the passage of fish is obstructed in this place, but if a huso got trapped in the V shaped weir, the mouth of the opening was closed with a net. Both illustrations make

35. Komoróczy (1932), pp. 18–25.

36. Lukács (1953), *passim*.

37. Unfortunately, the original document could not be found in the Public Record Office of Budapest. Ascertaining exact data regarding topography and the use of chained hooks would have necessitated a close scrutiny of this document. Szamota refers to Fasc. 49 of the "Nádasdy Archives" in the Public Record Office, but the numbering has since been altered. Its style marks the text at issue as having formed part of some farming account; however, a survey of the Nádasdyana accounts in the Record Office proved of no avail, and it was impossible to go through all the 44 bulky volumes of the Nádasdy collection. Russian incendiary projectiles set fire to the building of the Public Record Office in Budapest during the Hungarian war of independence in October–November, 1956, and the collection in question was destroyed, so the problem can no longer be solved.

Isolated cases of hooks' being suspended by means of chains do not justify far-reaching conclusions. The idea of attaching iron chains to large hooks may arise independently in disconnected remote areas. This is so natural that it would be superfluous to refer to Bastian's ethnological principle, known as the fundamental principle of *Elementargedanke*. It can be added that chained hooks are in general use for the purposes of sea fishery.

38. Donau Ansichten (1826), picture 226; text, pp. 38–39.

39. *Ibid.*, picture 247; text, p. 39.

it clear that the dam or weir, as used by Danubian fishermen, served only to stop the passage of fish, while their capture remained the task of the fishers. Dragnets were used on the middle Danube presumably from prehistoric times through the Middle Ages up to the nineteenth century, while seine nets and rows of hooks seem to have been employed around the Iron Gate in J. Alt's time.

The row of hooks described by Heckel at the middle of the nineteenth century from the area of the Iron Gate also appears to have consisted of anchorshaped units. He reports that when the huso had managed to pass beyond the weirs,

they encountered further upstream a wall of thousands of burnished sharp hooks, half a foot high, which were suspended by means of ropes of differing lengths from a common strong rope across the Danube.... When the movement of the signs, applied to the ropes, shows that the sturgeon are playing with the hooks, the fishermen row up to them silently, give a sudden pull to the ropes, and often one or the other sturgeon, while swimming above the hooks, gets caught and is captured by the fishermen. And, even if this powerful animal succeeds in evading the glittering hooks and continues his path upstream, while stirring up the rich mud of the Danube, nets are ready to catch it.[40]

The dimensions mentioned in Heckel's text allow no definite conclusions as to the shape of the hook. Both anchor-shaped and one-branched hooks may have had a length of about half a foot. The sudden jerking-up of the main line, as mentioned in the description, points to the use of anchor-shaped hooks, which were better suited for this operation.

Neither does the description reveal anything about the boundary between the region of hooks and that of nets. Conjecturally, it may be said that above the cataracts of the Iron Gate huso was caught by means of nets and not as yet with hooks.

Writing of present-day fishery as practiced by Serbian fishermen in the region of the Iron Gate, Petrović remarks that besides one-branched sturgeon hooks "some may have two prongs." The latter have a length of a span, are made of forged iron, and are usually manufactured in the workshops of village gypsies.[41]

A communication of A. Khin reveals the fact that chained, anchor-shaped huso hooks were also used at Csallóköz, the largest island in the middle stretch of the Danube between Pozsony and Komárom.[42] Khin also said that hooks of this kind were in use in this area only until the middle of the last century and that fishermen of our day did not remember this technique.

Anchor-shaped huso hooks were still in use at Dunapentele (below Budapest) at the end of the last century. Three large hooks were hammered together and a wire was wound round their necks so as to hold them together. A float made

40. Heckel (1863), p. 212.
41. Петровић (1941), p. 75.
42. Khin (1936), p. 42.

of willow bark (originally intended for nets, called *stupli*) was drawn over the shank (Fig. 9). Rows consisting of such hooks were then placed across the river.[43]

A revival of anchor-shaped huso hooks occurred in comparatively recent times in the Serbian portion of the Danube; sterlet hooks of this description were set up near the village Sip in the twenties of our century (Fig. 10).[44] The

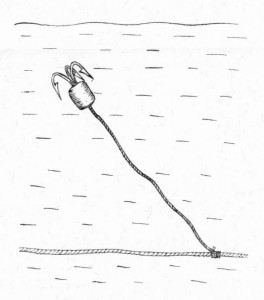

FIGURE 9.—Anchor-shaped huso hook at the end of the nineteenth century. Dunapentele, middle Danube. (Reconstructed from the oral description of fishermen.)

manner of their suspension was like that described by Herman in connection with chained huso hooks. Every other hook of the row was single-branched. Since these sterlet hooks were light, their float was, of course, different from that of huso hooks. They were, moreover, more submerged than huso hooks. The line was attached to two signal pumpkins, and each hook also had a separate float, which was similar to the floats used for huso hooks and was not merely a simple piece of cork, as was the usual float of the sterlet hooks.

Anchor-shaped, industrially manufactured sterlet hooks were in use at Mohács thirty years ago (Fig. 11). These were considerably smaller than huso hooks and were made from thin steel wire. Their barbs, in the conventional shape of industrially manufactured hook, formed an outward arch. The float— not willow bark in this case but the sort of cork used for beer bottles—was applied to the neck of the hooks in quite the same manner as in the case of the earlier huso hooks of Dunapentele. Also, these sterlet hooks were provided with the pumpkin (Fig. 12) seen in Libay's map, but the pumpkin served here

43. Information received from a seventy-year-old fisherman (József Gulbint) of Dunapentele in autumn, 1951.

44. Zega (1926–27), p. 40.

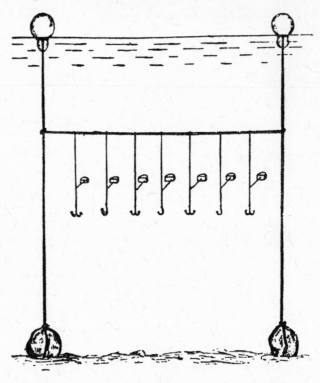

FIGURE 10.—Anchor-shaped sterlet hooks. Sip, south of the Iron Gate, lower Danube (After Zega.)

FIGURE 11.—Anchor-shaped sterlet hook (about 1930). Mohács, middle Danube. (Reconstructed
from the oral description of fishermen.)

merely as an indicator, because the small hook could not be tied below the
pumpkin, which, if employed as a float, would have hampered it. Sterlet hooks
are usually let down almost to the bottom, and their float is correspondingly
deeply submerged, whereas the float of huso hooks swims on the water's

surface and serves at the same time as indicator, so that no special object (e.g. the pumpkin) is needed for this purpose.

The anchor-shaped sterlet hook of Mohács was in use for only a few years and was never universally adopted.[45]

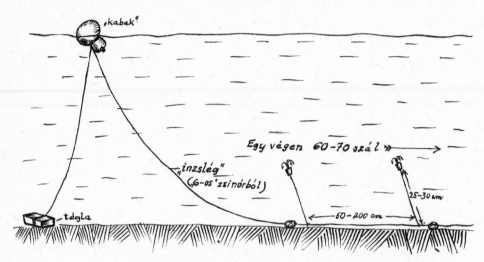

FIGURE 12.—Anchor-shaped hooks set up for the fishing of sterlet (about 1930). Mohács, middle Danube. (Reconstructed from the oral description of fishermen.)

By way of summing up this information regarding anchor-shaped huso hooks, it can be said that such pieces were still used as single hooks around the Iron Gate and on the Balkan Danube at the end of the eighteenth century and likewise were employed in the delta of the Danube prior to World War I. It is safe to assume that the use of anchor-shaped single huso hooks was once general along the entire Balkan portion of the river. The manner of their manipulation was the same as that described by Aelianus, and even the bait seems to have been similar. This points to the existence of a continuity in fishing technique since antique times, with the sole difference, however, that one-branched hooks were presumably used in antiquity and were later replaced by the two-, three- and four-branched, anchor-shaped varieties.

Rows of serially arranged anchor-shaped hooks represent a comparatively recent development, although such devices were already known to the fishermen of the Iron Gate region at the outset of the nineteenth century, as witnessed by J. Alt's lithographs. The reports of Heckel and Herman make it evident that this serial arrangement had become more general by the middle of the century.

Toward the turn of the century the lighter tridentate hooks appeared; those used for huso had floats of willow bark, and the smaller sterlet hooks pieces

45. Information regarding anchor-shaped sterlet hooks employed at Mohács was given in May, 1954, by Ignác Angyal (fisherman of Mohács, fourty-two years old) and Mihály Takács (fisherman of Mohácssziget, sixty-two years old).

of cork. These anchor-shaped hooks, by having the floats drawn over their necks, came to lie in the water in that reversed position which is the character-istic feature of samolovs.

5. HUSO HOOKS SUSPENDED FROM PILES

A. Khin provided information about a less-known technique of huso angling as practiced in the Csallóköz area.[46] Two parallel rows of piles were driven into the river bottom across the current so that the piles of one row were behind the gaps formed by two adjacent piles of the other row. The head of each pile emerged from the water, and the line of the hook was attached to it. The polished hook hung down into the water and the current threw it to and fro (Fig. 13).

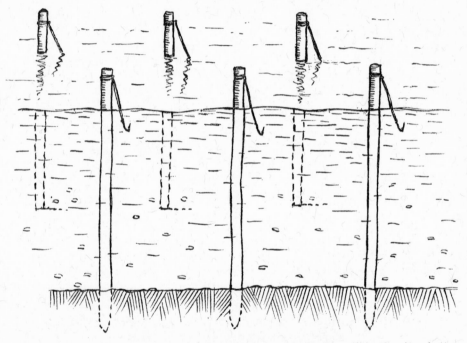

FIGURE 13.—Huso hooks, each of which was attached to a pile driven into the river bottom (middle of nineteenth century). Csallóköz Island, middle Danube. (After Khin.)

Khin was the son of a master fisherman in the Csallóköz, and his father had met fishers who still employed this technique at the middle of the last century. This type of huso hook was apparently the first to have traveled from the southern part of the Danube to its middle stretch.

Such an arrangement of the hooks seems to be rather primitive and is reminiscent of fishing with solitary huso hooks. The whole system is a kind of

46. Khin (1936), p. 42.

transitory form between fishery by means of single hooks and fishery using a row of hooks attached to a transverse rope.

The significance of this row of hooks fastened to piles lies in the fact that no other similar system is known. But for the conviction that Hungarian fisherman were ignorant of huso hooks prior to the eighteenth century, one would be inclined to think that such huso hooks were first applied to the weir that consisted of two rows of beams and was destroyed at Komárom in the nineties of the sixteenth century, so the technique in question might have represented a survival of that earlier system.

6. CONTROVERSIES REGARDING THE ANALOGY BETWEEN DANUBIAN AND EASTERN EUROPEAN HOOKS OF THE SAMOLOV TYPE

In the discussion of the Danubian anchor-shaped huso hooks reference was made to a similar medieval tool from southern Russia. Although a connection between the two cannot be doubted, the time and circumstances of the process of transmission, on the one hand, and borrowing, on the other, is not known. There is, however, ample information about the eastern European origin of those structurally more primitive hooks of the samolov type that were first developed in the Russian river systems and have recently been adopted by Danubian fishermen.

Visiting the international exhibition of fishery at Berlin in 1880, O. Herman, while inspecting the Russian exhibits, was surprised to see a type of sturgeon hook that seemed to be an exact replica of the hooks used at that time by fishermen along the Danube as far up as Dunaföldvár. He writes of this discovery with his customary enthusiasm:

There was, among the fishing tools as used along the Volga, an admirable hook which served for the fishing of the great sturgeon, and whose exact replica is to be found along our fair Danube that used to be so rich in huso at the time of Marsilius [L. F. Marsigli] and is so depopulated nowadays.

It is an approximately span-sized, powerful, needle-sharp hook whose *patony* [the short and thin rope which connects the main line and the hook] is a decent piece of rope and its *in* or *horogderék* [main line] is not less so either; the poplar or willow float is attached to the hook, and the main line carries 120 to 200 such hooks as are illustrated in Fig. 106 [see our Fig. 14].

This long tool was put across the water in several rows in the Volga and the Danube alike; it was sunk into the water so that, naturally, the hooks were floating in the current. There was no bait on the hooks, nor was this necessary since the swimming piece of wood suffices to arouse the attention of the passing huso or sturgeon. Mistaking the float for a piece of foodstuff, it snaps it up and spits it out again; disappointed, it flies into a rage, whisks its tail, knocks it against one of the hooks and comes to grief. It is mostly with their tails that these giant fish get caught, and it is astonishing that, although the hook does not penetrate beyond the skin, this powerful ancient animal keeps still, does not tear itself away, as if all creatures had been more sensitive in those prehistoric times from which these giants derive.[47]

47. Herman (1887), I, 216–17. Fig. 106 as mentioned in the quoted text is on p. 216.

Herman gives no geographical indication, but it can be safely assumed that he describes a scene at Apatin, for the same figure is contained in the catalogue of an exhibition arranged by him in Budapest in 1885, and Apatin is indicated as the place of provenance in the explanatory text.[48]

FIGURE 14.—Huso hook of the samolov type, suspended from float. Apatin, middle Danube. (After Herman.)

The following passage is taken from that part of Herman's book which enumerates prehistoric fishing analogies: "The manner in which the Russian sturgeon *(Acipenser sturio)* is caught in the Caspian Sea is the same as that in which Hungarian fishermen catch huso.[49] He refers in the footnote to a picture and its description in the report on the Berlin exhibition.[50] The reference is, however, wrong, because the report did not contain all the materials of the exhibition. It depicted precisely that variety of Volga huso hooks which bore the least resemblance to those used in the Danube. The hooks in the report are shown hanging down from the line, while the Danubian hooks are lifted above the line by the wooden float. It should be noted that—as will be seen later—the collection of the Budapest Ethnographical Museum includes a specimen on which the hooks are suspended from the line. It was found by Herman long after the appearance of this book.

J. Jankó, in sharp issue with Herman, pounces on this erroneous reference and—after enlarging upon the difference between the two hook types—attacks the aged scientist violently:

48. Herman (1885), p. 46; Fig. on p. 17.
49. Herman (1887), I, 146.
50. Amtlicher Bericht (1881), II, 162.

How did Herman's error arise? A careful scrutiny of the three drawings mentioned convinces me that Herman's error was once more due to that contemptuous superficiality with which he treated his western sources. He must have omitted reading the text; otherwise, he could not have failed to notice that he was dealing not with an exact copy of the Hungarian huso hook but with a tool which—according to Herman's book, at least—does not exist in Hungary in any form. He contended himself with looking at the picture only and he did even that in a perfunctory manner....

It is perhaps needless to add that this Berlin picture is a reproduction of a page from Danilevskij's album; if Herman had seen that album he would really have found a genuine counterpart, "an exact replica," i.e., a true analogy, of the Hungarian huso hook. This tool is in general use on the Volga; it is well known and has already been represented by Gmelin in both writing and drawing, although his drawing is primitive and partly erroneous since the floats are on and not below the water's surface.[51] This tool is known in Russia under the name *samolov* (самоловъ) and is used not only for sturgeon but also for all kinds of large fish, especially for sterlet, in various sizes.

Jankó goes on to prove "the impossibility" of Herman's "genealogization" and continues: "We are interested in the origin of the tool above all, and we must really look for it in the valley of the Volga." He then discusses the geographical distribution of the samolov in Russia, a subject that will be treated later in this essay (see Chap. IV, sec. 3). After this, he analyzes its origin:

That it is not of Ugrian origin is proved by the fact that neither the Ostyaks nor the Finns use it. It might be Turko-Tatarian or Russian. We are not in a position to decide the problem but have to remember that the *samolov* is not known everywhere in Russia and that the Russians settled along the Volga during the last centuries only. If we consider these factors, we are inclined to come to the conclusion that the hook at issue was borrowed by the Magyars from the Turko-Tatars and not from the Russians, and that it must have happened in the Volga region. This theory seems to be substantiated by Munkácsi, who demonstrated[52] that the words *horog* (hook) and *böncső* (hook-stone) were of Turkish origin.[53]

By way of summing up, Jankó says:

We can see that, although it was impossible for Herman to infer this identity from the picture on page 162, Vol. II, of the book on the Berlin exhibition, he has unwittingly hit upon the truth, and all we have to add is that the huso hook is of Turkish origin.[54]

Otto Herman, offended in both his person and his self-respect, confesses on the reading of János Jankó's book that he committed an error. He acknowledges that the picture referred to by him represents a huso hook suspended from a line and not a floating one. He goes on to argue that the Danubian

51. Gmelin (1774–84), II, 212; Pl. 38.
52. Munkácsi (1893), p. 48.
53. Jankó (1900), pp. 519–22.
54. *Ibid.*, p. 580.

huso hook is nevertheless the same as the samolov, so that his reference to
the analogy from the Volga was justified after all. He says he made the reference because he knew the trick of how to set up the hook so as to make it
"catchy." In conclusion, Herman excuses himself by pointing out that he did
refer to a hanging huso hook at the end of his book, that is, to the "chained
hook," which is set up quite like the one figuring in the Berlin memorial
volume, with the sole deviation that the shape of the individual hooks is
different.[55]

Looking back at the polemic of the two Hungarian scientists of European
fame from a distance of a half-century, one does not understand why Jankó
felt induced to start a debate with Herman. Surely the latter's claim was
justified: the huso hook used on the Volga was perfectly similar to that of the
Danubian fishermen, both morphologically and structurally, and only Herman's reference was erroneous. He inspected the objects exhibited in Berlin,
and it was there that he must have seen huso hooks with wooden floats in
natura or in pictures. It was there that he must have concived the truth, but,
in writing his book, he seems to have preferred a reference to a literary source
instead of substantiating his statement by merely recalling what he saw at the
exhibition. Having in mind the image of a hook seen there, he mixed it up
with another kind of picture—that contained in the memorial volume. That
this supposition is not fanciful is proved by Herman's explanatory text, which
refers to the exhibits seen in Berlin and not to the memorial volume of the
exhibition. Herman would never have discovered the identity of the Volga
and Danube hooks if he had contended himself with limiting his attention to
the sole principle of "catchiness." He must have actually seen the Volga hook,
that is, the original object, since otherwise he could not have been so sure of
the alleged identity. At least twenty years had elapsed between the date of
the exhibition and the appearance of Jankó's book. Herman, in the heat of
the debate, was aware only of his actual mistake—his erroneous reference—
and no longer remembered what he had seen twenty years before. However,
the fact remains, and it cannot be doubted, that it was Otto Herman who
discovered the analogy between the Danubian and the eastern European
huso hook.

Note in connection with Jankó's lines quoted above that Gmelin's representation is not erroneous. The floats of the huso hooks used on the Volga in the
eighteenth century swam on the surface of the water quite as did those of the
Danubian hooks. Jankó knew only the more recent, and smaller samolovs,
which were in truth more submerged than the original type.

7. MIGRATIONS OF FISHERMEN AS FACTORS IN THE DISSEMINATION OF SAMOLOV HOOKS

Having discovered the Russian analogy of the huso hooks in the course of
his investigations into the "prehistoric elements" of fishery, Herman expressed

55. Herman (1900), pp. 87–88.

his view that the Hungarians had adopted these hooks prior to having occupied the Carpathian Basin in 895 A.D. Jankó shares this view but adds that the Magyars of the Völkerwanderung "borrowed it [the hook] not from the Russians but from the Turko-Tatars, undoubtedly somewhere in the Volga valley."

This monograph will prove that the Magyars did not borrow the huso hook from the Turko-Tatars, and certainly not in the Volga region.

Although Jankó knew Danilevskij's most important works quite well, he unfortunately did not read the latter's report on the exhibition of fishery held in Paris in 1867: "When the delta of the Danube belonged to Russia, fishing centers were established there on the model of the fisheries of the Caspian Sea, and fishermen, as will as experts on caviar and ichthyocol, were settled in this area." Danilevskij adds that this was the most prosperous era of fishing along the lower Danube.[56] Had Jankó been aware of this report, he would surely have approached the analogies between Russian and Danubian fishing methods with more care, for it is clear that the adoption of fishing tools, working methods, and their associated terminology may have happened not only during the migration of the Magyars across the steppes prior to their settlement in the territory of the later Hungary but during subsequent centuries as well.

The Danube Delta has thus a key position, not solely with regard to the dissemination of the sturgeon hook but also with regard to relationships between Central European and Eastern fishing methods. It therefore seems necessary to present a brief survey of the great migrations of southeastern and Central European fishermen. The most significant of these movements are the settlement of Lipovan fishers in the Danube Delta and the stream of Volga fishermen to the Black Sea and later to the delta of the Danube.

First to be mentioned is the settlement of Ukrainian (Little Russian, Malorussian, or Hahol) fishermen around the estuary of the Danube. Abounding in fish, this region had from time immemorial, attracted Ukrainian fishermen, who must have been led to this area though the direct waterways. The first pertinent record dates from the twelfth century: the so-called *Annals of Hipatius* refers to Ivan Rostislavevič in 1159, who is said to have harmed the interests of the Galician fishermen in the Danubian towns.[57]

One of the most important migrations toward the Danube Delta during recent centuries was that of the Lipovans. This movement was due to the reform of the Greek liturgy and the revision of Evangelical texts as laid down in 1655 by Nikon, patriarch of Novgorod. The reform was not accepted by all members of the Greek church. The conservative elements made violent protests, but Tsar Alexei Mikhajlovič dealt severely with them and squashed local insurrections. This started a great emigration that lasted about two centuries. Refugees from all parts of the Russian empire overflowed the delta of the Danube, which was under Turkish rule.[58]

56. Danilewsky (1867), p. 30.
57. Bobk (1899), p. 33.
58. For historical details see the bibliography in Bouillet's encyclopedic work.

The refugees called themselves "Lipovans". This is the adjectival form of the Russian word *lipo*, which means "lime tree." The explanation given by them is that they fled to lime-tree woods during their persecution by Peter the Great, who reigned from 1682 to 1725.[59] They were, at the same time, called *raškolnik* (i.e. schismatics) in Russia, a name applied to all kinds of emigrants).

The Lipovans are divided into numerous religious branches and sects. The most important group is that of the *staroveri* or *staroobrjadci* (who are orthodox), and a side branch of this group is that of the *popovec* (who have a priest); these are the Lipovans proper. But all the various fanatic and less extreme sects are to be found in the Danube Delta. Although they keep sharply separate and almost all of them have their own churches, they are collectively known as Lipovans.[60]

The members of the *popovec* sect are mostly of central Russian origin, those of the *bezpopovec* sect (who ignore any kind of clergy) hail from Russia's more northern regions, while several sects who call themselves "spiritualists" come largely from southern Russia. The latter include the sect of *stundists* (who pray at a definite hour), of Ukrainian origin.[61]

It can be seen that the word "Lipovan" serves only to distinguish a religious denomination and that the individuals so designated really form an ethnic hodgepodge. One finds among their ancestors muzhiks of the Russian steppe as well as Cossacks from the Don, Kuban, Dnieper, and Volga.[62]

The next wave of emigrants to arrive at the Danube Delta (1775) was that of the Ukrainian fishermen; about eight thousand Cossacks of Zaporozhe fled from the Sič (an estuary of the Dnieper) to this region, refugees from the despotic rule of Catherine II. They stayed at the estuary of the Danube until 1785; when they began to clash with the Lipovans they accepted the invitation of the Hungarian authorities and settled on the banks of the Tisza River in the Bánát (southern Hungary). However, they failed to strike roots in this place also and returned to the Dobrudja (to Seimen, beside the Danube), whence they migrated first toward Caterlec in 1813 and then to Dunavec.[63]

The last great wave of emigrants to arrive at the delta of the Danube was that of the Cossack Lipovans who came from the estuarial regions of the Don in the middle of the nineteenth century. According to tales told by their ancestors, they were forced by horrible acts of cruelty to leave their ancient abode. Many of them were, for instance, slain along the upper stretches of the Don, and the heads of the victims were thrown into the water by the executioners so as to frighten the Cossacks who lived along the lower stretches and at the mouth of the river. This induced 20,000 Don Cossacks to set forth toward Turkey under the leadership of their ataman, Nekrasov. Some of

59. Hosmer (1940), p. 416.
60. Pittard (1902), pp. 108–9.
61. Bouillet (1893), p. 1597.
62. Arnaud (1935), p. 24.
63. Вовк (1899), p. 33; Antipa (1916), p. 744.

them then settled around the Danube Delta in the towns Tulcea and Ismail (Nekrasovka), and also in the adjacent villages.[64]

Another large-scale migration that deserves mention in connection with the dissemination of hooks of the samolov type was that of the Volga fishermen, who wandered toward the east in quest of fishing places on the shores of the Black Sea; this region, though abounding in fish, was poorly exploited at that time. Fishing in the Meotis, so significant in Hellenic times,[65] underwent a gradual decline, for—according to Danilevskij—fishery on a larger scale in the Sea of Azov started only in comparatively recent times, and a hundred years ago it was still largely inferior to that in the Caspian Sea. Fishing activites around the mouth of the Volga took an upward swing as far back as the sixteenth century, when this region was occupied by the Russians. In those times there was practically no fishing in the Sea of Azov, and it was taken up only after Russian rule of the Don estuary had become definitely established (1769). It was in the nineties of the eighteenth century that fishery on a larger scale started in the Black Sea, when this region was settled also by the Zaporozhian Cossacks, who took refuge there for the reasons mentioned earlier. The northern littoral of the sea was still an uninhabited desert at the beginning of the nineteenth century, and it is a merchant from Berdjanks, by the name of Kobozev, who may be regarded as the owner of the first large-scale fishery in this region.[66]

Thenceforth, Volga fishermen began to settle on the shores of the Sea of Azov in increasing numbers. The reasons that induced them to choose this region instead of moving to the Caspian Sea were, according to Danilevskij, the following: (a) fish fetched higher prices there; (b) fishing was free at most places in the Azov littoral; (c) wages paid to fishermen were higher here; (d) fish were more abundant in the Sea of Azov so that fishermen could better spread along its shores; and (e) fishermen staying on the slopes and the shores along the Sea of Azov could live in the houses of the merchants ("hosts") who forwarded the fish, and, when the fishermen unloaded their tools, they did not have to remain long absent from their families.[67]

The expansion of the Russian Empire toward the delta of the Danube coincided with the rapid development of Russian industrial fishing methods, and the exploitation of fishing possibilities advanced at such a rate that the northern shores of the Black Sea were incapable of keeping pace with the steadily increasing demands. The Peace of Bucharest (1812) marked the Kilia branch as Russia's boundary, but the Tsar succeeded in acquiring also the Sulina branch through the Treaty of Akkerman in 1826, while three years later the Treaty of Adrianople extended his rule over the southern, that is, the St. George branch, so that the Tsar was now lord of the entire Danube

64. Antipa (1916), p. 742.

65. In order not to anticipate a later detailed analysis, reference is made only to Strabon's descriptions.

66. Данилевский (1871), p. 9.

67. *Ibid.*, p. 188.

Delta. That fishing interests lay behind this expansion is illustrated by the fact that no works necessary for the improvement of shipping were undertaken. The mouth of the river at Sulina filled up with mud, although the Russian government had—in the Agreement of 1840 with the Austro-Hungarian Empire—pledged itself to prevent such a contingency. It was therefore only natural that the Paris Treaty of 1856 deprived Russia of its Danubian possessions and allotted the Danu be Delta to Rumania.

The Russian fishing establishments had reaped rich benefits from this region. A noteworthy feature of this water system is that it is richer in huso than in any other variety of sturgeon. Stellate sturgeon and Russian sturgeon constitute the majority in the affluents of the Azov and Black seas, while the number of stellate sturgeon (the most frequent variety in the Sea of Azov[68]) is so low in the mouth of the Danube that it makes up hardly a tenth of the sturgeon caught there. The quantity of Russian sturgeon caught in the delta of the Danube equals that of the huso, but their weight amounts to no more than a fifth of all sturgeon varieties caught in this area.[69] The fact that the largest fresh-water fish of the world occurs here in such quantities elevates Danubian fishery to especially high rank.

In consideration of these circumstances, it will be understood why the fishermen of the Volga Valley not only acquired the neighboring fishing places but also went to more distant regions, to the ichthyofaunally rich places of the Black Sea and to the Danube Delta in particular. Of significance are those further transmigrations that the great entrepreneurs of Astrakhan seem to have organized at the very first annexations. The earlier migrations were spontaneous movements of fishermen and had, therefore, an organic character, in the course of which the emigrants carried to their new settlements and introduced there their traditional tools and methods of small-scale fishery. The later transmigrations had an organized character, in the course of which the emigrant fishermen received the most up-to-date fishing tools from and were taught the most recent working methods by their employers, who had acquired the lease of the new fisheries. Details in this respect belong mostly to a sphere beyond the limits of ethnography.

It can be presumed that the very first immigrants from the Dnieper and the Don brought to the Danube Delta that archetype of the Russian huso hook, the samolov, which was still in general use along the Volga during the eighteenth century. This hooking device was—perhaps under the influence of the Tatars living around the delta of the Danube—called *carmac*, a term that has survived until our own time. The hooks (claws) of the *carmac* of those times were called *daldon*: these large hooks were made of forged iron and are now gradually being replaced by more up-to-date forms.[70]

It is interesting that it was not the Russian word *samolov* but the Turko-Tataric word *carmac* that came into use for the huso hook among the two

68. *Ibid.*, p. 8.
69. *Ibid.*, pp. 304–5.
70. Antipa (1916), p. 334.

peoples who possess the major part of the Balkan Danube—the Rumanians and the Bulgarians. The Rumanians have adopted even the words that designate the constituent parts of the huso hook. The float is known as бабилка[71] at Astrakhan and as балбера[72] in the Ob Valley (i.e., the same word without the diminutive suffix), while the word *bulber*[73] is used in Rumania. The Russian word for the line connecting the float and the bend of the hook is силок,[74] and its Rumanian equivalent is *casilca*.[75]

According to Petrović, a prominent investigator of Serbian fishing methods, these rows of hooks must be of Turkish origin, for they were known by the Turkish name *takumi* along the Serbian portion of the Danube.[76] He claims that the fishing culture of this region was founded by Turks, who were the first to trade in the great sturgeon.[77] It is thus justifiable to assume that it was through the Turks that Serbian fishermen adopted the use of the ancient Russian sturgeon hook, the samolov. Note that Ada-Kaleh Island on the Danube, a center of Danubian fishery in the region of the Iron Gate, was under Turkish rule even at the beginning of the present century; it was reannexed by Hungary in 1908, after a foreign rule of four centuries, to be acquired thereafter by Rumania in 1919 under the Treaty of Trianon. The number of Turkish fishermen on the island is still considerable.

The establishment of Ukrainian and Russian fisheries, while giving a new impulse to fishing activities in the lower Danube, wrought radical changes in fishing methods. The new colonists imported their traditional Russian forged-iron hooks, and the passage of the great sturgeon ascending from the Black Sea was blocked by rows of such hooks between the second half of the seventeenth and the middle of the nineteenth century. This type of hook was then disseminated along the whole length of the lower Danube. This is the type that was described by Herman, and the classification presented in a later part of this monograph deals largely with the different varieties of this type.[78]

After two centuries, during which the *carmac*—composed of *daldons*, that is, the traditional Russian samolov—had been in use on the lower Danube, a new type appeared, one introduced by the fishermen of the Volga. This equipment consisted of smaller, industrially manufactured serial huso hooks suspended from a line. This was likewise called *carmac*, to which the memorial volume of the Berlin exhibition referred, and this gear formed the subject of the controversy between Herman and Jankó described earlier.

The date at which the new type of huso hook appeared is accurately known. Širokov, a fishing tenant new of Astrakhan, introduced the system of serially

71. Gmelin (1774–84), II, 212.
72. Варпаховский (1898), p. 41.
73. Ghelase (1951), p. 145.
74. Шульц (1861), p. 46.
75. Antipa (1916), p. 319.
76. Петровиђ (1941), p. 75.
77. *Ibid.*, pp. 79–80.
78. See sec. 9. of Chap. III.

suspended sturgeon hooks. As a lessee of the Danube Delta, he practically monopolized fishery in this area from 1840 to 1846. He hired skilled Astrakhan fishermen and earned vast profits during the six years of his lease by means of the new imported type of fishing gear. "Before, *daldons* served as fishhooks; these differed, in the main, from the new hooks in that they were much larger and were suspended from side ropes ('small reins') which had a length of 1 aršin and 6 veršok [i.e., 96,5 cm. and thus nearly a meter], with a distance of somewhat more than an aršin [i.e., 71.1 cm.] between them. The set line was lying on the bottom and the hooks pointed upward, a position in which they were kept by means of wooden floats."[79]

The *daldon* was then manufactured by Rumanian smiths on the analogy of hooks imported from Ukrainian and Russian rivers.[80] Since Rumania remained under the political and economic influence of Russia even after the delta of the Danube had ceased to be ruled by the Tsar, it is quite possible that Rumanian fishermen continued to import their sturgeon hooks from Astrakhan or the famous hook market of Rostov. This theory is advanced on the strength of the fact that a certain *carmac* is still known as "Astrakhan *carmac*" in the Danube Delta[81] and also on Danilevskij's statement[82] that samolov-like hooks were sold at Rostov for fishing not only in the Don but also in the Sea of Azov and even the Black Sea. These, too, were gradually replaced by a lighter type of hook imported from Great Britain.[83] The *daldon* seems to have survived both the Russian products of the last century and the more recent British hooks, since it was still in use in the Danube Delta at the time of Antipa's investigations.[84]

The tsarist authorities tried to prevent the rapid spread of sturgeon hooks both here and in other parts of the Russian empire. According to Danilevskij, the use of hooks was prohibited at the mouth of the Danube in the 1830's; he adds that this prohibition was never respected.[85]

Although the hook of the samolov type is practically the only tool used for huso fishing along the entire length of the Danube, the center of its application has always remained the delta of the river. Fishery in these parts is still practiced by Ukrainian and Russian fishermen. Although these fishermen are of very different origins, they can no longer be distinguished from an ethnic point of view, and their present division into separate groups follows religious lines only. The term "Lipovan," once covering a wide range of ethnically different people, means nowadays a more or less homogeneous ethnic group.

The exact number of Lipovans inhabiting the lagoons of the Danube Delta is not known. It was estimated at 13,200 by Pittard in 1902, who presumably

79. Данилевский (1871), p. 305.
80. Antipa (1916), p. 20.
81. *Ibid.*, p. 335; Ghelase (1951), pp. 146–47.
82. Данилевский (1871), p. 166.
83. Antipa (1916), p. 20.
84. *Ibid.*, p. 334.
85. Данилевский (1871), p. 299.

based his estimate on Rumanian official statistics.[86] Silverstru's official figure, determined a generation later (in 1936), was 15,800.[87] Arnaud, writing in the same year and apparently basing his estimate on data obtained from Antipa himself, stated that the number of Lipovans was not less than 30,000 and that they constituted four-fifths of the delta's total population.[88] Their capital is Vâlcov (Russian: Vili), with a population of 8,000, Lipovans being the overwhelming majority.[89]

Owing to its extraordinary abundance of fish—and huso in particular—and also to its geographical and ethnic features, the delta of the Danube constitutes an especially important area of ethnographic research concerning European fishery. What the delta of the Volga meant for an ethnographic exploration of the Caspian littoral, the delta of the Danube meant for ethnographic research concerning the Black Sea. As the Volga's abundance of fish influenced the course of the Great Migrations to no small extent,[90] so did the Danube induce many people to seek a new home along its banks during the Völkerwanderung[91]. As the fishermen of distant regions used to assemble at Astrakhan in the past century,[92] so did, more recently, a multitude of Ukrainian, Russian, Turkish, Tataric, and Greek fishermen assemble in the delta of the Danube.[93] The entire Dobrudja side of the Danube, from Silistra downward, was still full of foreign fishermen prior to World War I.[94] All these people, coming from remote lands, brought and retained their traditional tools, fishing methods, and old customs.

86. Pittard (1902), pp. 47–48.

87. Silvestru (1936), p. 118.

88. Arnaud (1936), p. 15.

89. Hosmer (1940), p. 428.

90. In this connection one thinks of a correct interpretation of the sources concerning the fishery of the Magyars in the first place, but also of those other (chiefly Bulgaro–Turkish) peoples who lived in and passed through this area during the Völkerwanderung. European ethnology could have drawn more far-reaching conclusions from available data if it had realized the significance of the great sturgeon migrations of southern Russia. By paying due attention to what the authors of antiquity said concerning these areas and also to those archeological finds that have been made in the meantime (a method of research initiated by J. Jankó, who began the comparison of recent central European and eastern European data), each particular method of fishing can be brought in line with the usages of the nomadic Magyars and a better insight can be had into their manner of life and into the factors that determined the course of their migrations.

Clark suggests that the annual run of Acipenseridae was one of the factors that contributed to the colonization of certain regions by the agricultural-stockbreeding peoples of the Neolithic Age (Clark [1952], p. 56). This suggestion, by the way, points to the existence of certain inherent laws and is supplemented by remarks of Marquart concerning the Hungarian nomadic population of southwestern Europe (southern Russia of the present time), in which their occupation with fishing is especially emphasized (Marquart [1903], pp. 40, 51 and 54). These and other similar sources have lead to the assumption that the geographical distribution of Acipenseridae might have constituted a factor determining the course taken by the migrating Hungarians in quest of a new *Lebensraum*.

91. Antipa (1916), p. 7.

92. Moynet (1867), pp. 82, 81.

93. Antipa (1916), p. 745.

94. *Ibid.*, p. 741.

This multicolored mixture of tools, methods, customs, and traditions has developed into a fairly complicated pattern of fishing culture on the lower Danube, which influences European fishery as a whole. There are many instances to prove the wide-reaching effect of lower Danubian fishing customs, and it cannot be doubted that the whole water system of the Danube has been greatly influenced by them. Apart from sturgeon hooks of the samolov type, a great number of other tools, working methods, and customs, introduced by the newly settled colonists of the delta, have been taken over directly or indirectly by fishermen along the entire length of the Danube. The effect of the fishing establishments of the delta on Danubian fishery in general can be said to have been revolutionary, but the details of this subject are too extensive to go into here.

It is an irreparable loss of European ethnology that J. Jankó failed to notice this process. Had he paid attention to it, no revision would now be necessary of his statements based on Russian and Turkish analogies, for it is certain that he would not have hesitated to analyze the structure and historical development of the lower Danubian fishery with his accustomed thoroughness. Had he done so, Antipa would have had no occasion to reproach Jankó for having searched for eastern analogies before familiarizing himself with the entire complex of the Danubian fishing culture.[95]

8. THE DISSEMINATION OF SAMOLOV HOOKS ALONG THE MIDDLE DANUBE

We have seen that the immigration of Ukrainian and Russian fishermen, induced partly by religious and partly by economic factors, was the significant historical event that gave rise to a radical change in the ethnic pattern of the lower Danubian fishing establishments. The movement in question was not merely a matter of seasonal migration but consisted of successive settlements and consecutive waves of new colonists have, of course, produced a permanent and strong influence. They introduced the Russian samolov, which came to be known as the *carmac*, and, according to Antipa, it was this type of hook that "replaced all earlier primitive Rumanian sturgeon-fishing tools."[96]

Antipa, unfortunately, fails to describe those earlier, "primitive" fishing tools. They undoubtedly included the sturgeon weir and the sturgeon net, which were in use also on the Hungarian Danube prior to the appearance of the samolov. In section 3 of this Chapter it was shown that no sturgeon hooks existed in the middle Danube and that huso was caught by means of weirs and nets up to the end of the eighteenth century. Since the huso weir had disappeared from the Danube above the Iron Gate earlier than had the huso net,[97] it was the latter that ceded its place to the new tool, the huso hook.

95. *Ibid.*, p. 7.
96. *Ibid.*, pp. 286–87.
97. The huso weir disappeared from the middle Danube at the end of the sixteenth and from the Tisza River at the end of the seventeenth century, while Serbian fishermen employed it up to World War I at the Iron Gate, near the village Sip.

The change occurred as early as the second half of the seventeenth century on the Balkan portion of the river, that is, below the Iron Gate, and the process was fairly rapid. The large huso weirs, damming up the river and its side branches, nevertheless remained there for some time. They played an auxiliary role by blocking the path of the fish, which could thus be caught more easily by means of nets ; only the latter—sack-shaped nets applied to the opening in the middle of the weir—continued to play the role of independent catching tools. When the hooks, suspended in several rows, came to be substituted for the nets, they were placed before the weirs.

The substitution of huso hooks for nets occurred much later on the Hungarian stretch of the Danube—about the middle of the nineteenth century. According to Heckel's report, huso were still caught with nets and not by means of hooks north of the Iron Gate in the forties of the last century.[98] Rómer records that the great sturgeon was already being caught with hooks at Apatin in 1866: "The hook is fastened to a black wooden ball which is tossed to and fro by the current; the huso begins to play with it, knocks against it with its tail, and impales itself."[99] A similar substitution of hooks for nets took place in 1920 with respect to the sterlet, another variety of sturgeon with properties similar to those of the huso. This subject will be dealt with in more detail in Chapter III, section 11 (pp. 62-64).

The spread of hooks of the samolov type along the Middle Danube was determined by two factors, one positive and one negative. The first was the regulation of the Iron Gate which opened the path for the spread of the huso-hooks towards the upper stretches of the river; the second was the gradual abatement of the seasonal migrations of the great sturgeon, which reduced the necessity of huso hooks.

Regular water traffic across the Iron Gate started a few years after 1837, and it is well known that shipping, or rather the boatmen, play an important part in the spread of fishing tools. Hooks of the samolov type were carried by them to the middle Danube from the lower portion of the river.

Investigators of fishery from an ethnographic point of view have found many instances to prove that boatmen are important mediators in the dissemination of certain fishing tools. This is especially true in the case of such large water-ways as the Danube. Most of the boatmen on these rivers are recruited from young fishermen, they spend the greater part of their lives on ships and barges and return to fishing in their old age. Boatmen usually do a bit of fishing during their journeys up- and downstream and also during the time of loading and unloading. In doing so, they pick up new tools and new methods here and there. The full description of this richly patterned "water life" would require a separate ethnosociological essay, but it will suffice here to point out that the large fishing centers of the middle Danube were identical with the large port towns situated along the river; Apatin, for example, was both

98. Heckel (1863), p. 212.
99. Rómer (1866), XXI, 1–2.

one of the most significant Danubian ports and one of the most important fishing colonies. It is therefore not by mere chance that the majority of the huso hooks to be exhibited in the collection of the Budapest Ethnographical Museum originated at Apatin, although many of them were actually manufactured at places along the Balkan portion of the Danube.

The negative factor that barred the further spread of huso hooks on the middle Danube was the cessation of the large fish migrations. Let us bear in mind that hooks of the samolov type arrived at the middle Danube (between Pozsony and the Iron Gate) precisely during the last phase of huso fishing on the grand scale, which had been flourishing since prehistoric times. In Chapter III, section 5, a description was given of the huso hooks that were hanging from rows of piles at Komárom; they were, however, but an isolated phenomenon. When the use of samolovs was adopted (in the second half of the nineteenth century) on the middle Danube, this new tool ousted the old one completely. The southernmost point of Csepel Island must have been the northern boundary of the seasonal sturgeon runs at the end of the nineteenth century. Accordingly, the last station of huso fishing was the area of Dunaföldvár. No regular huso fishing took place north of this portion of the Danube.[100] No shoals of the great sturgeon swam farther northward; only a few isolated individuals got above this portion, and hooks of the samolov type did not spread further to the north, since there was no need for them. By 1880, the time of Herman's field work, even the fishermen of Komárom had ceased to operate with hooks suspended from piles and returned to the use of the ancient net on the rare occasions when thus was huso fishing.[101]

It was thus the discontinuance of the migration of the giant fish that prevented the spread of samolovs north of Dunaföldvár. The absence of the great sturgeon in those places was due to an excessive use of huso hooks along the Balkan portion of the Danube, which simply made it impossible for the fish to travel farther north. Antipa's words help present an adequate picture of the truly unrestrained use of huso hooks at the beginning of the century. He says that "millions of hooks" (daldon, provided with floats) were swimming in the water over a stretch of about ten miles above the mouth of the Danube, so that any kind of shipping was impossible there.[102] The uninterrupted and reckless devastation greatly reduced the number of sturgeon. This forest of hooks was almost impassable for the fish, and less and less frequently could an occasional smaller individual fish manage to reach the middle Danube.

Great sturgeon had completely disappeared from the middle Danube before the outbreak of World War I. This meant, of course, the simultaneous falling into disuse of hooks of the samolov type after an employment of about six decades. Somewhat later, however, there appeared (after 1920) a smaller variety of the samolov, the sterlet hook.

100. Leist (1865), p. 199.
101. Herman (1887), I, 281.
102. Antipa (1916), p. 320.

9. TYPOLOGY OF RECENT DANUBIAN HUSO HOOKS OF THE SAMOLOV TYPE

The collection of the Budapest Ethnographical Museum has been used in establishing the following typology of Danubian huso hooks. The original stock of this collection, unique of its kind, consists of the objects assembled by Herman for exhibitions arranged between 1884 and 1900. The present collection included ninety-eight Danubian huso hooks, eight of which were lost during the cataclysm of World War II. Most of the hooks are provided with float and cordage, and almost all are painted with tar.

This outstandingly significant collection contains a wide variety of differently shaped fishhooks. Most of them were collected by Herman at Apatin, whither they had been brought by boatmen who were plying the river down to the Black Sea. This explains the variety of the collection. It is safe to affirm that the hooks originated in various places along the lower and middle Danube, so the collection may justly be claimed to represent all important variants of the sturgeon hook that were in use along the entire length of the Danube during the nineteenth century. This being so, classification of the Danubian huso hooks herein has been based on the collection of the Budapest Ethnographical Museum.

The establishment of a morphological series is by no means equivalent to setting up a genealogical sequence, but it would be wrong to disregard differences that point to the historical chronology of the objects.

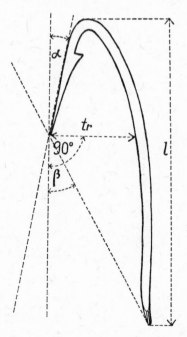

FIGURE 15.—Size index determining the character of sturgeon hooks of the samolov type. (After Ghelase and de Rohan-Csermak.)

In addition to photographs of the objects presented here, a constructional design drawn according to the modified scheme of Ghelase[103] is given (Fig. 15). The longitudinal scale represents the standard scale of all museological publications. For the transversal scale the distance between the inner line of the shank's curve and the point of the hook has been chosen instead of the outside diameter. This is the characteristic dimension of the hook, since it is this distance that plays the important part in catching the fish. Angle α indicates the bend of the crook. That the crook is always straight and pointing outward is a characteristic feature of huso hooks, which distinguishes them from all other types. Angle β is actually a supplement to the transversal measure and shows likewise the open or closed position of the crook. It is not necessary to indicate the length of the crook separately, since it depends on angle β: the larger the crook, the wider will angel β become. Herman raised the principle of the "catchiness" (effectiveness) of hooks and of fishing tools in general. He reminded ethnographers that it was not enough simply to register objects and their use; the degree of their effectiveness should also be noted. So that readers may form a more accurate idea of morphological features, instead of mere general descriptions, comparable numerical data will also be presented.

Type I (Pl. VI, No. 1; Fig. 16)[104]

The collection of the Budapest Ethnographical Museum contains only a single hook in the Type I category. Its bulky and crude appearance stamps it at first sight as archaic. It has two conspicuous characteristics:

(a) the shank is massive and its section quadrate, and

(b) the hook is unbarbed.

That the shank has a square-shaped section, that is, that the hook is a curved, four-edged iron bar, indicates an ancient technique of manufacture. In an earlier publication[105] I demonstrated that this morphological feature pointed to a more remote age than that of hooks with a circular cross section. The other archaic feature, the absence of a barb, needs no explanation; that plain hooks belong to the remote past is well known among ethnologists,

The hook in question is a piece representative of the ancient *daldon* discussed in section 7 of this chapter. It is possible that its provenience was precisely the area of the Danube Delta. The *daldon* described by Antipa (Fig. 17), which was still in use at the mouth of the river when he was writing his book, is similar to the hook at issue. Its section is likewise square, but its shape is more suggestive of recent industrially manufactured hooks. It is 15 centimeters long, and it is, according to Antipa's explanatory text, "the oldest type of *carmac* that has been employed in the delta of the Danube"; we learn also

103. Ghelase (1951), p. 140.
104. Inventory No. of the Budapest Ethnographical Museum: 134.958–7.
105. Cf. de Rohan–Csermak (1959), p. 11.

that its smithing is crude and that it is less curved than the usual type of huso hook.[106] All these features apply to our hook as well.

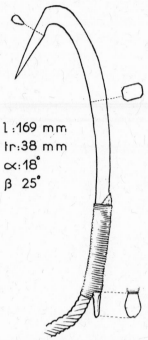

l :169 mm
tr:38 mm
∝:18°
β 25°

FIGURE 16.—Huso hook of Type I. Danube. (In the Budapest Ethnographical Museum.) For photograph see Plate VI, No. 1.

Type II (Pl. VI, No. 2, and Fig. 18; Pl. VII, No. 1, and Fig. 19)[107]

Hooks of Type II can be said to form a transition from the most primitive type to somewhat more elaborate forms. Though transitory, this type nevertheless reveals certain independent features.

While the four-edged shank and the plain (unbarbed) point appear in their pure form in Type I, these characters are only vestigial in Type II. The shank of the hook is coarsely forged; although still four-edged, the edges are less distinct, so that hooks of this type almost constitute a transitory form to hooks with cylindrical shanks. The point of the hook is quite like that of Type I; but, while the inner line of the crook is straight between the bend and the point in Type I, there is a markedly protruding barb in Type II. This barb is different from that seen in other types of huso hooks inasmuch as the point is turned upward instead of downward, which is the usual position of sturgeon hooks. This construction reveals the fact that the barb, as seen in Type II, was intended not to prevent the hook from slipping out of the body

106. Antipa (1916), p. 334.
107. Inventory Nos. of the Budapest Ethnographical Museum: 5.850 and 134.958-2.

of the fish but rather to fix the attached float line. This arrangement helped
to preserve the narrow point of the hook.

The circular curve of the shank is noticeable in all types of the huso hook,
and especially in Type II as presented here. This feature differs from the

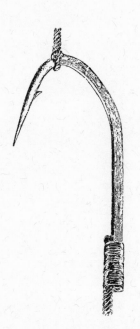

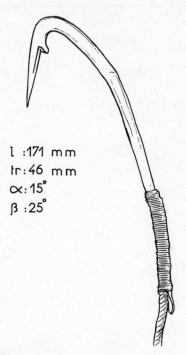

l :171 mm
lr:46 mm
∝:15°
ß :25°

FIGURE 17.—Daldon of archaic design for
huso fishing. Danube Delta. (After Antipa.)
Length, 15 cm.

FIGURE 18.—Huso hook of Type II. Apatin,
middle Danube. (In the Budapest Ethnographical Museum.) For photograph see Plate
VI, No. 2.

straight shank of modern Danubian hooks and suggests prehistoric origin.
Herman also noticed the ancient character of hooks with curved shanks: he
dated them from the earliest Iron Age.[108] Similarly arched shanks of mesolithic
hooks (to be discussed below) and also a similar feature observable in some
of the recent Finnish wooden hooks seem to prove that this traditional characteristic has an origin earlier than the Iron Age. The shape of the wooden hooks
especially points to the "lignic" culture of the Paleolithic. Clark, through
a different way of reasoning, arrives at the same conclusion: he thinks that
certain fishing tools, the oldest of which are dated from the neolithic culture,
may have arisen in the Upper Paleolithic.[109]

108. Herman (1887), I, 179.
109. Clark (1952), p. 42.

Type III (Pl. VII, No. 2, and Fig. 20)[110]

Type III. Hooks have very long and crudely forged shanks, while their point is carefully executed and smoothly polished. They have three principal morphological features:

(a) The outer line of the point is curved and not straight.

(b) The section of the point, instead of being circular, is in the shape of a water drop turned toward the inner bend. The entire point is thus flattened, so that a blunt edge on its inner side runs from the barb to its end.

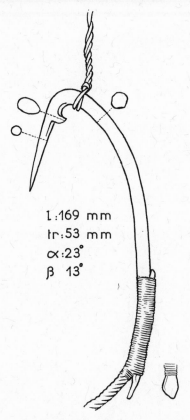

L:169 mm
tr:53 mm
∝:23°
β 13°

FIGURE 19.—Huso hook of Type II. Danube. (In the Budapest Ethnographical Museum.) For photograph see Plate VII, No. 1.

(c) The inner curve of the hook forms a complete semicircle after the barb. This type of barb, which, instead of being incised at a right angle below the point, continues in a long arch into the line of the inner curve, affords an interesting comparison. This shape of the barb shows a conspicuous similarity to northern mesolithic hooks and also to the neolithic hooks of the Central European lake dwellings.

110. Inventory No. of the Budapest Ethnographical Museum: 134.958–1.

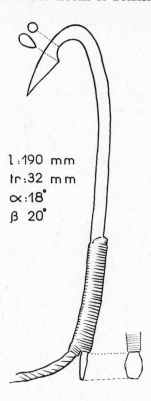

l : 190 mm
tr : 32 mm
∝ : 18°
β 20°

FIGURE 20.—Huso hook of Type III. Danube. (In the Budapest Ethnographical Museum.) For photograph see Plate VII, No. 2.

FIGURE 21.—Semifinished drilled bone hook from the Neolithic. Gåsen, near Stavanger, Norway. (After Clark.)

FIGURE 22.—Fragment of drilled semifinished bone hook from the Neolithic. Viste, near Stavanger, Norway. (After Brøgger.)

FIGURE 23.—Drilled bone hook from the Neolithic. Östergötland, Sweden. (After Clark.)

Maglemosean man was the first to use a drill when shaping his fishhook. By doing so, he formed a primitive barb on the hook.[111] This "dodge" (the expression used by Clark to describe the use of drills) survived in the European neolithic culture, but its analogy can be traced to remote continents also. Applied to bone hooks, this technique gave rise to a characteristic new form, which is represented by the type of huso hook under review.

The prehistoric process of preparing fishhooks with a drill is observable in the semifinished hook which was found at Gåsen, near Stavanger in Norway (Fig. 21).[112] A likewise semifinished hook that seems to have been broken during manufacture is described by Brøgger (Fig. 22).[113] A whole series of finished bone hooks from Scandinavia is described by Gjessing[114] and Clark.[115] Figure 23 shows a specimen from Östergötland (Sweden)[116] that conveys a good idea of the construction that should be regarded as the precursor of the perfected barb seen on metal hooks. The hooks of the lake dwellings of Switzerland must have been made with the same drilling process as their northern analogies, as can be seen on the staghorn hooks of the palafittes and numerous bone hooks from the Lake of Constance[117] (one of them represented in Fig. 24),[118] from the boar-tusk hooks found at Moosseedorf near the Lake of Bern (Fig. 25),[119] and from the staghorn hooks of Lattringen.[120] Especially noteworthy among the *néolithique lacustre* hooks is the boar-tusk hook unearthed at Nussdorf near the Lake of Überlingen (Fig. 26)[121] which is like our huso hook in respect to its exterior curve and is likewise similar to the semifinished hook of Gåsen described above.

Morphological comparisons become still more fascinating if we go further afield in quest of similarities; the neolithic bone hooks of Lake Erie[122] and those found in Japan[123] likewise show the technique of drilling.[124] Many more instances could be adduced, but it is not proposed to give a complete list in this presentation. All that needs to be demonstrated is that the type in question had a fairly wide distribution at an early stage of its evolution. Considering the earliest finding places, the geographical distribution, and the

111. Clark (1952), p. 42.

112. Clark (1948), p. 62, Fig. 10, No. 8.

113. Brøgger (1910), p. 22.

114. Gjessing (1945), p. 117, Fig. 23, Nos. 4–9.

115. Clark (1948), p. 64, Fig. 11, Nos. 7–9; p. 66, Fig. 12, No. 1; p. 67, Fig. 13, No. 5.

116. Clark (1948), p. 66, Fig. 12, No. 1.

117. Krause (1904), p. 219, illustration: Pl. XI, No. 347.

118. R. Munro (1890), p. 126, Fig. 27, No. 16; Krause (1904), p. 219, illustration: Pl. XI, Nos. 348 and 349.

119. Krause (1904), p. 219, illustration: Pl. XI, No. 350.

120. Nougier and Robert (1951), p. 315, Fig. 5, No. 4.

121. R. Munro (1890), p. 140, Fig. 31, No. 22.

122. Rau (1884), p. 126, Fig. 188.

123. N. G. Munro (1911), p. 101, Fig. 27, No. 2.

124. ([1952], p. 42) also mentions in this connection the hooks from Santa Cruz and New Zealand pictured in Rau's book ([1884], pp. 129–37), although these are shark hooks and so quite different (cf. Gudger's publication, which contains rich material).

richness of the finds, it is safe to assume that the original center of hooks of this type was western Norway. It must have been via the arctic passages that the hook in question was carried to North America and the still more remote Japanese waters.

A comparison of Type III with the analogies given above shows that, not only the arc of the inner bend, the triangularity of the point, and, in some

FIGURE 24.—Drilled bone hook from neolithic lake dwelling. Lake of Constance, Switzerland. (After Munro.)

FIGURE 25.—Drilled hook made of boar tusk, from neolithic lake dwelling. Moosseedorf, Lake of Bern, Switzerland. (After Krause.)

FIGURE 26.—Drilled hook made of boar tusk, from neolithic lake dwelling. Nussdorf, Lake of Überlingen, Switzerland. (After Krause.)

instances, the curved line of the outside, but also the characteristic shape of the shank point to a relationship with mesolithic and neolithic bone hooks. Such morphological similarities cannot be due to mere chance. Data concerning the arctic origin of huso hooks (see *infra*) make it especially certain that this type of Danubian huso hook is a morphological survival of mesolithic traditions.

Type IV (Pl. VIII, No. 1, and Fig. 27; Pl. VIII, No. 2, and Fig. 28)[125]

It seems certain that Type IV evolved from Type III. The section of the point is likewise shaped like a waterdrop, but this type has a perpendicular incision at the corner of the barb so that the bend of the hook is not semicircular as in the preceding type. Barbs perpendicular to the crook mean a transition to the next type, and the transitory character of hooks of this type is also revealed by the size of the shank. The most characteristic feature of hooks of Type IV is that the lateral view of the point shows an elongated isosceles.

125. Inventory Nos. of the Budapest Ethnographical Museum: 32.982 and 33.144.

Type V (Pl. IX, No. 1, and Fig. 29; Pl. IX, No. 2, and Fig. 30; Pl. X, No. 1, and Fig. 31; Pl. X, No. 2, and Fig. 32)

Type V, directly developed from the preceding type, is most amply represented in the collection. Seen in profile, the point is not a regular triangle, since the line connecting the corner of the barb with the point of the hook is concavely arched. The point becomes, accordingly, narrower than in Type IV, and its section, still oval at the barb, is circular near the end.

The length of the crook is also greater in this type, as is clearly indicated by the higher index of angle β. Tools of this type, with their "needle" point,

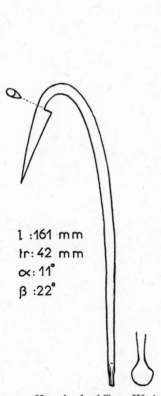

l :161 mm
tr: 42 mm
∝: 11°
β :22°

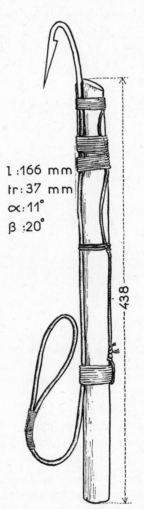

l :166 mm
tr: 37 mm
∝: 11°
β :20°

438

FIGURE 27.—Huso hook of Type IV. Apatin, middle Danube. (In the Budapest Ethnographical Museum.) For photograph see Plate VIII, No. 1.

FIGURE 28.—Hafted crook (gaff) forlifting fish caught with huso hook of Type IV. Apatin, middle Danube. (In the Budapest Ethnographical Museum.) For photograph see Plate VIII, No. 2.

are true sturgeon hooks, whose manipulation requires more circumspection. The flattened end of the shank does not always have the circular form caused by rough hammering but shows in some instances the shape of a heart or a triangle. We first encounter hooks prepared from industrially produced wire in this type, which, however, were still hammered into their final shape by smiths.

The huso hook[126] presented in Plate IX, No. 1, and Figure 29 is evidently the work of a smith. The end of its shank is heart-shaped.

Plate IX, No. 2, and Figure 30 show a huso hook made from wire;[127] the end of the shank is triangular. It may have been manufactured by a smith,

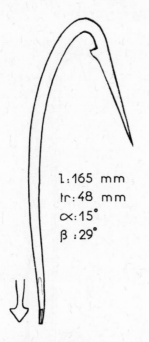

l:165 mm
tr:48 mm
∝:15°
β :29°

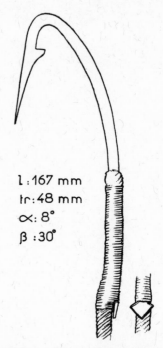

l:167 mm
tr:48 mm
∝: 8°
β :30°

FIGURE 29.—Forged huso hook of Type V. Apatin, middle Danube. (In the Budapest Ethnographical Museum.) For photograph see Plate IX, No. 1.

FIGURE 30.—Huso hook made from industrial wire. Tolna, middle Danube. (In the Budapest Ethnographical Museum.) For photograph see Plate IX, No. 2.

who seems to have bent the machine-made wire and hammered it on an anvil. The huso hook represented in Plate X, No. 1, and Figure 31 appears to have come from the same workshop.[128]

A fourth variety of Type V[129] is shown in Plate X, No. 2, and Figure 32. The flattened end of the shank forms an irregular circle.

126. Inventory No. of the Budapest Ethnographical Museum: 32.984.
127. *Ibid.* 54.39.16.
128. *Ibid.*: 33.115.
129. *Ibid.*: 33.173.

It should be noted that there is practically no structural difference between the varieties of Type V; they seem to have been modeled according to a common pattern. It was only in the flattening of the shank's end that the smith was free to give rein to his idiosyncrasies. This enables us to tell which hooks were made in the same workshop, so the form of the shank's end may be regarded as a sort of signature of the artisan.

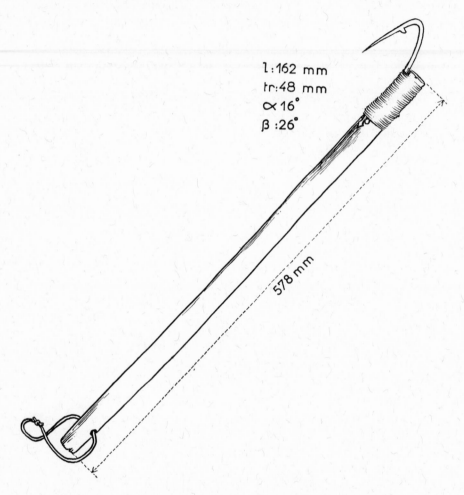

l : 162 mm
tr : 48 mm
∝ 16°
β : 26°

578 mm

FIGURE 31.—Hafted crook (gaff) for lifting fish caught with huso hook of Type V. Apatin, middle Danube. (In the Budapest Ethnographical Museum.) For photograph see Plate X, No. 1.

Type VI (Pl. XI, No. 1, and Fig. 33)[130]

Even a mere glance at the picture makes clear that the point of these hooks is excessively long in comparison with the shank, as revealed also by the fact that angle β is 50 degrees. Another noteworthy feature of this type is that, in contradistinction to other types, the curve of the shank does not form

130. In the Budapest Ethnographical Museum, without number.

the usual line, which begins with a slight arc and is then bent by a sharp twist. The bend is broader here and has two breaks, a moderate and a sharper one. The hook is made from industrially manufactured wire, but the incision of the barb reveals the hand of a skilled smith. The barb of the preceding type was hammered white the iron was red-hot, whereas here the barb must have been incised into the cooled iron, a little from the side. Unusual and indicating a technique different from that employed for the manufacture of Danubian hooks is the fact that the end of the shank is not flattened; it conveys the impression that it is unfinished.

Hooks of Type VI are identical with the "hooks of Astrakhan" used by Rumanian fishermen in the Danube Delta (Fig. 34)[131] which reveals their probable origin. This probability becomes certainty if we inspect sturgeon hooks employed in the Volga River and the Caspian Sea.[132] These agree with our sample not only in shape but also in that the shank seems to be cut off at the end. They are likewise floatless, because the hooks are suspended from

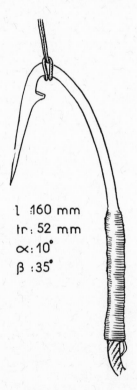

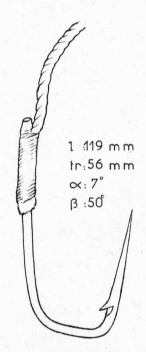

l 160 mm
tr: 52 mm
∝: 10°
β : 35°

l 119 mm
tr: 56 mm
∝: 7°
β : 50°

FIGURE 32.—Forged huso hook of Type V with float. Danube. (In the Budapest Ethnographical Museum.) For photograph see Plate X, No. 2.

FIGURE 33.—Hanging floatless huso hook made from industrial wire, Type VI. Danube. (In the Budapest Ethnographical Museum). For photograph see Plate XI, No. 1.

131. Antipa (1916), p. 337, Figs. 148–49.
132. Шульц (1861), Рисунки . . ., Pl. A IV.a, Fig. 2, and Pl. A IV.a, Fig. 1.

the main line to catch the huso. This is the type of hook represented in the memorial book of the Berlin exhibition to which Otto Herman made his erroneous reference. And this is the hook that replaced—first in the Volga and then in the lower Danube—the traditional *daldon*, that ancient forged hook whose varieties constitute Types I-V discussed above.

Type VII (Pl. XI, No. 2, and Fig. 35)[133]

Without doubt, hooks of this type are of Russian origin. This is proved by the threefold break of the shank, which, as will be seen, is a characteristic feature of hooks used along the Ob River.

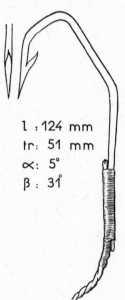

l : 124 mm
tr: 51 mm
∝: 5°
β : 31°

FIGURE 34.—Hanging floatless huso hook, called "Astrakhan hook," Type VI. Danube Delta. (After Antipa.)

FIGURE 35.—Industrially manufactured huso hook of Type VII. Apatin, middle Danube. (In the Budapest Ethnographical Museum.) For photograph see Plate XI, No. 2.

The arched excision of the barb from the surface of the wire is factory work and could not have been made by an individual smith. That this is so is revealed also by the zinc plating, which imparted a silvery shine to the new hook. Crook and shank are nearly parallel. Its smaller size shows that hooks of this type must have been used in that period of huso fishing when, owing to systematic massacre, the large individuals of the great sturgeon had already disappeared so that the traditional large hooks had become superfluous. The fact that none of the specimens of the collection is provided with a float permits the conclusion that they were suspended from a main line as were hooks of the preceding types.

133. Inventory No. of the Budapest Ethnographical Museum: 5.989.

Type VIII (Pl. XII, No. 1, and Fig. 36)[134]

The hooks of this type were acquired by the Budapest Ethnographical Museum in 1954. The history of their arrival at the middle Danube is known; they were brought from Pancsova (now Pančevo) to Mohács at the turn of the century by József Agócs, a fisherman who had also served as a boatman for some time. The shape of these hooks is essentially different from that of the classic huso hooks. The bend of the crook, turned inward rather than outward, shows that hooks of this type must have been made in factories. The fishermen using such hooks could not have been completely familiar with the "tricks" of the trade, since, otherwise, they ought to have known that crooks bent outward are better for huso fishing. The length of this type hardly reaches half that of the old huso hooks, thus proving that only degenerate successors of the quondam giant fish reach the regulated middle Danube from the Black Sea.

Hooks of Types VI and VII, still regarded as novelties not so long ago, are now superseded by those of Type VIII, and it is chiefly with these hooks that Rumanian[135] and Bulgarian[136] fishermen catch huso passing upstream.

A new technique is observable also in the manner in which the line is twisted round the shank of these recent hooks. Yet Antipa's illustrations (Figs. 37 and 38) prove that the line was sometimes attached to the shank in the tradi-

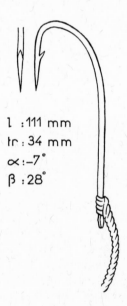

l : 111 mm
tr : 34 mm
α : –7°
β : 28°

FIGURE 36.—Industrially manufactured huso hook, Type VIII. Mohács, middle Danube. (In the Budapest Ethnographical Museum.) For photograph see Plate XII, No. 1.

134. Ibid.: 54.39.20.
135. Antipa (1916), p. 328; Ghelase (1951), p. 140.
136. Андреев (1922), p. 125.

tional manner even on these small hooks. The trapezohedral floats of an early period, made from the thick bark of willow, are replaced by cylindrical corks, large bottle stoppers, or—according to a Bulgarian source—barrel plugs.[137]

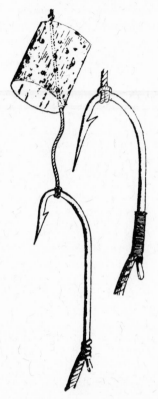

FIGURES 37 and 38.—Huso hooks of Type VIII, provided with cork. Turtucaia-Silistra, lower Danube (After Antipa.)

10. CHANGE IN THE FUNCTION OF DANUBIAN HUSO HOOKS

Let us now see what purpose the huso hooks served after the cessation of the great sturgeon migrations. A pathetic tale is told by old fishermen at Mohács and Tolna of how difficult it was for them to become resigned to the cessation of the rich annual hauls and how they kept trying and trying again to make use of their familiar fishing gear. It was impossible for them to forget the rich hauls of their youth, although these were as nothing compared with the carloads of huso caught by their fathers. Although the rows of hooks had ceased to yield any result, they made new attempts every year, hoping that a few sturgeon might perhaps still oblige by getting caught. These attempts continued as long as the unimpaired hooking tackle kept on hanging in the cubbyhole or under the eaves; seeing it, the fisherman was unwilling to

137. *Ibid.*, p. 125.

leave it idle. However, after some time, the ropes wore out and it was no longer worthwhile to repair them. Huso hooks became just so much scrap iron and remained so until the day when a good housewife found out that these discarded hooks were excellent for hanging cured meat. "Sic transit gloria mundi": the once redoubtable enemy of the Danube's giant fish landed in the chimney or attic to serve the peaceful purpose of bearing the weight of cured bacon and ham.

After the disappearance of the great sturgeon, there remained only one large species in the middle Danube, the sheatfish. To lift the sheatfish from the water and haul it into the boat, a so-called *vágóhorog* ("cutting hook" gaff) is required, that is, a hook provided with a handle. Huso hooks were eminently suited for this purpose, so the neglected powerful iron hooks came into use again wherever a hunt for sheatfish was practiced. The sample seen in Plate VIII, No. 2, and Figure 28, a "cutting hook," shows the ingenious manner in which Danubian fishermen applied this obsolete tool. The ropes hanging from the hook can be used to form a loop at the end of the handle, which, being directly attached to the hook, offers more security. The sample shown in Plate X, No. 1, and Figure 31 shows that the hook is fastened to the handle by just two nails driven into the flattened end of the shank, so that it was necessary to reinforce the attachment by windings that helped to fasten the hook more closely to the handle. The loop, to be attached to the wrist of the fisherman grasping the handle, was passed through a hole, as is usual in cutting hooks.

The float of the huso hook also underwent a functional change. Thickly tarred willow bark was excellently suited for use as a float for nets. However, the hole through which the thin float line was passed was too small to allow the passage of the thicker line of nets. It was therefore necessary to pierce a second, larger hole, making it possible to utilize this auxiliary part of the old huso hook too.

II. APPEARANCE OF STERLET HOOKS OF THE SAMOLOV TYPE ON THE DANUBE

After the turn of the century it was still worth while for the Rumanian and Serbian fishermen to await the seasonal run of the great sturgeon with adequately set-up huso hooks, while baitless samolovs with floats had become remnants of the past for fishermen dwelling along the middle Danube.

Although huso hooks retained their usefulness in the lower stretches of the Danube (below the Iron Gate), a similar but smaller type, the sterlet hook, became popular also. Sterlet hooks were likewise introduced by Russian fishermen to the lower Danube, though much later than huso hooks. The exact time is not known but it was only a few decades ago that this type arrived at the middle Danube (i.e., the portion above the Iron Gate).

Hungarian fishermen became acquainted with the sterlet hook after 1920 through the mediation of boatmen. It is known that boatmen like to spend their free time fishing for their midday or evening meal. Fishing is really a sort of secondary profession of boatmen, and many of them pursue these two occupations alternately. According to information collected from Hungarian fishermen, Rumanian boatmen were the chief disseminators of the sterlet hook, but Hungarian boatmen, too, had opportunities of becoming directly acquainted with this cheap fishing tool when their boats were loading or unloading at ports on the lower Danube. The time of the diffusion of sterlet hooks was presumably the twenties and thirties of this century. No exact date can be named, for sterlet hooks did not spread by degrees; they emerged at different places, as is natural if they were imported by boatmen.

Two kinds of tools were used for sterlet fishing before the adoption of hooks; osier weels were employed in some places,[138] but the use of nets was more general. The sterlet net had three layers, consisting of a fine-meshed net between two coarse-meshed ones. Herman[139] described the sterlet nets used at Komárom and Budapest. They are still in use at the former place, and neither their size nor the manner of their manipulation has changed since 1880. Since the appearance of sterlet hooks[140] after 1920, the significance of nets has gradually declined.

Sterlet in the Tisza River was, according to Herman, likewise caught with nets. They were called *regyina* nets and resembled those used by the Danubian fishermen of Komárom.[141] Herman does not write of hooks in this connection, but, half a century later, Ecsedi points out that nets have become rare on the Tisza[142] and that only "ground-hooks" are used for sterlet fishing by Tisza fishermen.[143] It seems that sterlet hooks of the samolov type, much more suitable for the desired purpose, had not yet reached this region, so sterlet was caught at this time by means of that earlier type of hook usual for catching sheatfish, pike, and *Aspius rapax*. The new type of sterlet hook made its debut at Szeged (lower Tisza) after 1920.

We can see that just as the huso net was replaced by the huso hook, so was the sterlet net replaced by the sterlet hook nearly a century later. Although use of the sterlet net has not yet been wholly discontinued, its days seem to be numbered since the appearance of sterlet hooks.

Observations made at Mohács will show the extent to which the spread of sterlet hooks of the samolov type is governed by south Danubian influences. They know two varieties of sterlet hooks at Mohács. One is that described in connection with anchor-shaped hooks, the other is the one-branched hook suspended from a cork. I encountered two fishermen who used the first and three who used the second type. All of them acquired their gear and learned its use directly from Rumanian or Hungarian boatmen who had returned

138. Osier weels of this kind for catching sterlet are still employed around Tokaj on the upper Tisza. Their construction resembles that of the ванда on the Volga, as will be noted in connection with the discussion of Russian samolovs (see sec. 2 of Chap. IV).

139. Herman (1887), I, 285, and II, 800.

140. Szurmay (1926), pp. 44–45.

141. Herman (1887), I, 283.

142. Ecsedi (1933), p. 207.

143. *Ibid.*, p. 172.

from the lower Danube. This shows that here the sterlet hook was not introduced by a single fisherman who taught his fellows how to use and handle the
new gadget.

Worthy of note is the observation that the memory of the old huso hook is
so vivid at Mohács that some fishermen still call the sterlet hook by the old
name of "huso hook." This confusion of names dates from the very first
time that the sterlet hook was used.

Sterlet hooks were first employed at the beginning of the thirties at Százha-
lombatta. The fishermen of this region learned their use from Rumanian
boatmen. Large hooks (huso hooks) were originally imported by the boatmen,
but small ones (sterlet hooks) came to be popular subsequently.

This type of hook has been the most important tool of a small fisher of
Paks ever since 1946. He adopted it from an old fisherman who had used it but
rarely. This informant has "perfected" the tool and employs a stronger line
and stronger hook than the original model.

The fishermen of Bogyiszló made the acquaintance of the sterlet hook
through a fellow of theirs from Baja; they tried the new gear but did not
find it satisfactory. It has been used at Baja for a number of years, and its
existence had been known earlier. As far as they can remember, it was first
brought there by boatmen. Fishermen from Baja were responsible for its
adoption at Érsekcsanád several years ago.

To show that the mere existence of the tool is not enough for its spread,
and that its general adoption depends on initiative and individual psychological
factors, the fishermen of Tolna may be cited. Many of them spent long years
on boats and had ample opportunity of observing and learning the use of
sterlet hooks on the Balkan portions of the Danube. Yet it did not occur to
any of them that this hook could be used with advantage in their native place
when they returned from their wanderings.

12. MORPHOLOGICAL AND STRUCTURAL VARIETIES OF THE DANUBIAN STERLET HOOKS

A sterlet hook is a hook of specific construction. Its structural principle is
identical with that of the huso hook, though it is smaller, as follows from the
different sizes of the two kinds of fish. A characteristic feature of middle
Danubian sterlet hooks is that each carries a separate float. The latter has
been described in connection with hooks of Type VIII (i.e., bottle stoppers
of cork or, as referred to by the fishermen, "beer-bottle corks"). The floated
hook is called *dugóshorog* ("corked hook") around Baja and *stoplis horog*
("stoppered hook", from *Stoppel*, "stopper" or "plug," in German) at Mohács.
Serbian fishermen call it *pampur* hook (*pampur* means the plug-shaped float).[144]

Three varieties are known. The first tallies with the one-branched huso
hook: a cork is attached to the bend of the shank that keeps the hook afloat.

---

144. Петровић (1941) p. 105.

This is the most widespread of the three varieties, and the hook itself is longer than in other types (from 4 to 6,5 cm.). It may come from the workshop of a smith but is usually a factory product.

The second variety has already been described and shown (Figs. 10, 11, and 12) in connection with anchor-shaped hooks. Not only anchor-shaped but also two- and even one-branched hooks with corks drawn over their shanks were used at Mohács. They are shorter than the first variety (4-5 cm.). Only factory-made hooks in commercial circulation constitute this category.

The manner in which the third variety is set up and used is different from what we have learned in connection with huso hooks. S. Szurmay saw how it was handled by fishermen of Gönyü and Komárom in the 1920's and de-scribed it in the following terms (Fig. 39).

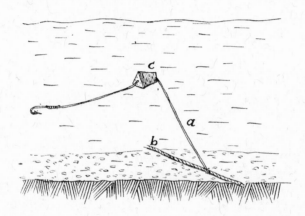

FIGURE 39.—Third alternative for setting up sterlet fishing gears. Gönyü and Komárom, middle Danube. (After Szurmay.)

The *horogpatony* (*horog* means hook and *patony* means the thin rope con-necting the main line with the hook) *(a)* is tied to the set line (the rope at the bottom) *(b)*. In order to prevent the hook from descending to the bottom, a frustum-shaped cork *(c)* is drawn over the *horogpatony* which—since its spe-cific weight is less than that of the water—lifts the line up so that the hook is floating about a span above the bottom. The triangular cork, met by the current in an oblique plane, is tossed about in the water and imparts its move-ment to the hook, which glitters while being turned about in the water. The sterlet, passing along, finds it, begins to play with it, and gets caught. Fisher-men at Gönyü and Komárom make rich hauls with such gear in the summer season.[145]

E. Solymos recently encountered a similar hooking device near Baja; in this arrangement, the cork drawn over the *patony* was only 2 centimeters below the hook.

145. Szurmay (1926), p. 45.

The third variety has the smallest hook. Szurmay speaks only of the measurement of the hook's bend: it amounts to 1-1½ centimeters, which would mean a hook 3-4 centimeters long. These hooks have to be small so as to remain light and easily movable by the stream.

Two of the sterlet hooks of the Budapest Ethnographical Museum are presented in this work. The first, as seen in Plate XII, No. 2, and Figure 40,

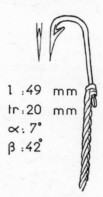

l :49 mm
lr:20 mm
∝: 7°
β :42°

FIGURE 40.—Forged sterlet hook; shows morphological traces of the sheatfish hook but is adapted to sturgeon fishery. Mohács, middle Danube. (In the Budapest Ethnographical Museum.) For photograph see Plate XII, No. 2.

reveals the traditional pattern.[146] One can see that it was made by a smith who had also produced sheatfish hooks. Its size, curve, and execution are in exact agreement with those seen in the sheatfish hooks used during the last hundred years (Pl. XIII, No. 1; Fig. 41),[147] with the sole difference that the

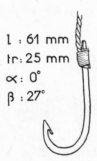

l : 61 mm
lr: 25 mm
∝: 0°
β : 27°

FIGURE 41.—Typical sheatfish hook, illustrating its similarity to sterlet hook as shown in Fig. 40. Tisza. (In the Musée de l'Homme, Paris.) For photograph see Plate XIII, No.1.

point is elongated, a form suited for catching sterlet. The bluntness of the barb makes it evident that its only purpose is to prevent the cork line from slipping off. It is the curve of the barb that particularly imparts grace to the beautifully worked hook. This piece is a good example of how a skilled smith

146. Inventory No. of the Budapest Ethnographical Museum: 54. 39.21.
147. Inventory No. of the Musée de l'Homme, Paris: 01.57.138–3.

is able to give the hook a traditional shape and yet make it suitable for sterlet fishing.

The second exhibit (Pl. XIII, No. 2; Fig. 42)[148] is a conventional factory

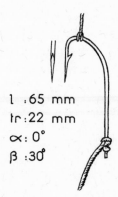

l :65 mm
tr:22 mm
∝: 0°
β :30°

FIGURE 42.—Industrially manufactured sterlet hook provided with cork. Mohács, middle Danube. (In the Budapest Ethnographical Museum.) For photograph see Plate XIII, No. 2.

product. The crook is parallel to the shank, which makes it less suitable for sterlet fishing. More instructive from our point of view is the adjustment of the cork through which the float line was passed obliquely. After the line had been passed through the cork, knot was tied in the end of it to prevent slipping. This knot was replaced by a small stick in some instances. Worthy of note is that only the cork is tarred, not the line. This sterlet hook is a miniature replica of the huso hook Type VIII.

148. Inventory No. of the Budapest Ethnographical Museum: 54.39.7.

CHAPTER IV

HOOKS IN EASTERN EUROPE

I. SOURCE OF THE WORD *SAMOLOV*

THE WORD *samolov* means automatic catcher. The complete term is самоловная снасть ("automatically catching hooking gear"), and only its abbreviated form is currently used. This parlance expresses the fundamental principle of the sturgeon fishing tackle—that it is baitless and that the fish catches itself on the hook. Samolovs, in this wider sense of the term, have two varieties: with and without float.

Of these two kinds, the historical—so to say "classic"—form is that described in ethnographic literature by Jankó and Manninen under the name of "samolov" and which was discussed in connection with Danubian Types I-V. To each of these hooks a float is attached by means of a short line so that the hooks will be kept afloat above the float line. This tool was, according to Pallas, called переметъ (now перемёт) in the 1870's along the Ob River; the word "samolov" was used only along the Irtysh River, while the hook in question was known as шашковая снасть on the Volga.[1] It is possible that the word *peremet*, which indicates nowadays quite another type of hook, was misinterpreted by Pallas, since the second volume of his travel book includes the statement that the sturgeon hook is generally called "samolov" in Siberia.[2] Varpakhovskij, writing of floated sturgeon and sterlet hooks used on the Ob River, mentions samolovs only[3] and distinguishes two kinds: the summer hooks and the winter юровой. The latter are somewhat smaller and are used on the Irtysh River.[4] Unfloated hooks—those hanging from the line—were apparently not used in the Ob Valley or anywhere in northern Russia.

Volga fishermen, on the other hand, know both varieties. Samolovs provided with floats, like those described as Danubian Types I-V, are called балберочная снасть,[5] балберочный крючок,[6] or шашковая снасть,[7] according to whether

1. Pallas (1771–76), III, 83.
2. *Ibid.*, II, 444.
3. Варпаховский (1898), p. 34 and *passim*.
4. *Ibid.*, p. 42.
5. Шульц (1861), p. 55.
6. Данилевский (1871), p. 166.
7. Kusnetzow (1898), pp. 29–30.

their float is балбера,[8] or шашка.[9] The first is the trapezohedral float that can be seen on the Danubian huso hook; it is used on the Volga for large huso and sturgeon hooks only. The second is smaller and plug-shaped, tied to smaller sturgeon and sterlet hooks. The word шашка designating this stopper-shaped float, is derived from the cylindrical figure in a game of draughts that used to be popular in Russia.[10]

The other kind of samolov, as used on the Volga, is a gear that has the hooks hanging from the line. Its Danubian representatives belong to our Types VI and VII. It should be noted that a combination of the two types has been evolved in the region of Astrakhan: every second hook is hanging from the line, and the intermediate hooks, provided with floats, are on the surface of the water.[11] This combined gear is also known on the Balkan portion of the Danube; it is called *perechi* ("paired") in Rumanian and двоснасть ("double hook") in Russian[12] (Fig. 76).

Rows of baited hooks of a character entirely different from the samolov are known as *peremjot* (перемёт or—an obsolete word—переметъ). These are not always hung downward from the line, and they usually carry a live fish as bait, so impaled on the hook as to remain alive as long as possible. The writhing bait-fish, trying to reach the surface of the water, pulls the hooks upward[13] so that the *peremjot* took, becomes a floating hook and remains so as long as the bait is alive. After its death, the hook of the *peremjot* will hang from the line as do hooks baited with pieces of flesh, grasshoppers, etc.

A functional difference between the *peremjot* and the samolov is that the latter is used only for Ancipenseridae and sometimes for sheatfish, while not only Ancipenseridae but also a great number of other fish are caught with the former.

2. THE RUSSIAN SAMOLOV IN MODERN TIMES

Of the investigators concerned with Russian fishery at the end of the last century Kuznecov can be said to have been ethnographically the best trained, and he was highly appreciated by Jankó.[14] He compiled a concise history of fishing in Russia, in which it is stated that in the sixteenth and seventeenth centuries the fishermen inhabiting the Kola Peninsula sued to sell the yield of their haul to Englishmen and Danes in exchange for linen, copper, and tin goods.[15] Although the document does not define the fish so bartered, it can be presumed that Acipenseridae are meant. Since the source in question allows the inference that fishery in the Kola region yielded rich hauls (its

8. Варпаховский (1898), p. 41.
9. Шульц (1861), pp. 140 and 40; Шульц (1861), Рисунки . . ., Pl. A IV.a, Figs. 3 and 4.
10. Ушаков (1939–41), III, 1325.
11. Шульц (1861), p. 45.
12. Antipa (1916), pp. 326, 336–37; Ghelase (1951), p. 142.
13. Шульц (1861), Рисунки . . ., Pl. A IV.b, Figs. 1 and 2.
14. Jankó's diary, II, 116.
15. Kusnetzow (1898), p. 5.

antecedents from the time of the Völkerwanderung and also a fossil bone
samolov unearthed in that area will be discussed in Chap. V, sec. 1), it is quite
possible that samolovs, eminently suited for the purpose, were used in sturgeon fishery at the time referred to be Kuznecov.

Only from the beginning of the eighteenth century have available Russian
sources explicitly described the existence of samolovs. Tsar Peter I issued
a ukase in 1704 prohibiting the use of samolovs anywhere in the empire except
in the Tsar's own fishing grounds. The reason stated for this measure was
that samolovs barred the passage of all kinds of fish in the rivers and that
samolov hooks caught small fry also. How popular the use of samolovs must
have been at that time is shown by the fact that the Tsar canceled his prohibition a year later and ruled that leaseholders of fishing grounds who wanted
to employ samolovs had to pay a supplementary fee over and above their
regular rent. Peter I seems to have been obliged to raise money by all possible
means because he was waging a war against Sweden and was, at the same time,
sending auxiliary forces to the king of Poland.[16] According to other sources,
the reason for the rescission was a reduction of rents received from leaseholders.[17]

Thereafter, the history of the Ob samolov has diverged from that of the
Volga samolov. Only samolovs furnished with floats were employed in the
basin of the Ob River,[18] and no information about floatless sturgeon hooks
is available. Acipenseridae were also caught by means of *peremjot* provided
with bait.

The situation is more complicated in the river system of the Volga, and
there the history of samolovs presents a more colorful picture. Huso fishermen
used both the samolov and the *peremjot* on the Volga in the second half of the
eighteenth century.[19] They used these two tools also in fishing for the smooth-
skinned sheatfish. The huso samolov балберочная снасть was the same as
the huso hook from the Danube described by Herman.

Sterlet was caught in the Volga at that time by means of a special sterlet
weel (ванда), the meshes of which were smaller than in other wickerwork
of this type. The sterlet fishers, who had the right to catch this fish during
the whole time of flood, were called вандовщик, a name derived from the
word ванда[20]. Osier weels were the only tools used for sterlet fishing, and
only larger varieties of the sturgeon were caught with weirs, nets, and hooks
on the Volga at this time.[21] The ванда was still in use a century later (which,
by the way, is suggestive of the central Russian wicker trap, крылен or
фитиль[22]), although by this time the special double-layered sterlet net had

16. Baer (1853), pp. 603-4.
17. Калебъ (1863), p. 67.
18. Варпаховский (1898), pp. 41-42.
19. Gmelin (1774-84), II, 213.
20. Lepechin (1774-75), I, 189.
21. *Ibid.*, p. 152.
22. Сабанеев (1892), II, 556.

already been adopted.[23] The latter seems to have become popular on the Volga in the seventeenth and eighteenth centuries, a theory convincingly presented by Jankó;[24] it was first used for various kinds of small fish. Sterlet fishers of the nineteenth century, however, used hooks almost exclusively. These sterlet hooks represented a smaller variety of the floated samolov, the шашковая снасть, furnished with the stopper-shaped шашка, which presumably arrived in the first of the nineteenth century from the Ob to the Volga. Coincidentally, the балберочная снасть was gradually superseded, either by the samolov with hanging hooks or the peremjot. In the middle of the last century Moynet saw nothing but such large hanging hooks, the main line of which was kept near the water's surface by huge timbers.[25] The members of the Baer-Danilevskij expedition encountered, at the same time, only samolovs with downward-hanging hooks instead of the swimming huso hooks described by Gmelin.[26]

The baited *peremjot* seems to have driven out both kinds of samolov from the Volga after the turn of the century and became thereafter predominant on the Kura River, another important fishing region of the Caspian Sea. Borodin's statistics show that 9,800 great sturgeon were caught in the Kura in 1901, 21,600 in 1902, and 20,300 in 1903. The annual haul suddenly dropped to 5,000-6,000 in subsequent years. Borodin attributes the temporary upswing in 1902-3 to the fact that the baited huso hook was adopted by Kura fishermen at that time.[27] According to recent information, the sterlet hook (шашковая снасть), as used in earlier times, is now prohibited in Russia. Only dragnets (swimming nets) are used for sterlet.[28]

The foregoing data are highly instructive in respect to central European conditions also. Evolution along the Danube and the Volga shows many similarities. It has been noted in connection with Danubian sterlet hooks that sterlet weels and sterlet nets had to cede their place to floating sterlet hooks on the middle Danube in quite the same manner as they did on the Volga a century earlier.[29] There was a similar exchange of nets for hooks in connection with Danubian huso fishing, as has been mentioned. It is interesting to note that the disappearance of floating huso hooks from the Volga coincided with their appearance on the middle Danube.

23. *Ibid.*, p. 556; Бэр (1860), p. 61.

24. Jankó (1900), I, 328–29.

25. Moynet (1867), p. 89.

26. Бэр (1860), p. 60.

27. Borodine (1913), p. 30.

28. Промысловые Рыбы (1949), p. 56.

29. A noteworthy instance of similarity is that existing between the sterlet weel still used at Tokaj (upper Tisza) and the ванда employed on the lower Volga (Шульц [1861], pp. 17–18, and Шульц [1861]—Рисунки. . ., Pl. A II.a, Fig. 7). Its significance is enhanced by the fact that the transversal rods are spiral, a scientific "tidbit," since, according to Jankó, a similar structure is unknown among either the Hungarians or the Finns, and is applied only among the Ostyaks of the Ob Valley (Jankó [1900], I, 195–96). Since Jankó's time its counterparts have been discovered in Finland, Estonia, and even in India. A more detailed treatment of the question would exceed the scope of this work.

Research into the origin of the "baited *peremjot*" used for huso in the Volga produces interesting results. Kuznecov, writing at the end of the last century, describes Turkoman fishermen catching the great sturgeon with a hook constructed from wood and iron to which a bream was laterally attached. These hooks were used singly as well as serially and in the latter case they were suspended from a common line.[30] Although this description appears to be of no special significance at first sight, it contains important information for us. The hook itself is akin to Finnish and Ostyak hooks, many of which are likewise bipartite, inasmuch as the shank is of wood while the attached crook is such of bone[31] or metal (copper and iron[32]). This construction leads us back to prehistoric hooks. A wooden hook will swim as it is, and becomes even more a floating hook if a live fish is attached to it. It needs only a step to arrive at the unbaited floating samolov hooks, where the wooden float itself serves as a kind of false bait.

That baits can be used as floats has already been discussed in connection with huso fishing as described by Aelianus. The floating bait, keeping the hook on the surface, was the lung of fattened cattle there, and it is live fish here. Another feature common to the huso hook of antiquity and that of Turkoman fishermen is its use as a single book. The fact that Turkomanic huso hooks were also employed in series, that is, attached to a common line, shows that similarly arranged rows of samolov and peremjot hooks derived from the single-hook type.

In connection with huso hooks mention must be made of the тычковая снасть, a tool used by the Caspian seal-hunters for catching huso under the ice. This is an uncommonly large hook of forged iron, two sizes of which are known. The smaller has a length of 5 verchok (22 cm.) and as shank of $\frac{3}{8}$ verchok (1,6 cm.); the larger is $7\frac{1}{4}$ verchok (32 cm.) long. After the leg or other organ of a seal has been attached to it, the hook is let into the water through a hole cut in the ice.[33] Although this hook does not belong to the samolov type, its shape and the manner of its manipulation make it akin to the samolov.

The use of seal organs for bait leads to the conclusion that the кусовая снасть may represent a later development of this hook. It is used by huso fishers of the Turkmenistan and Krasnovodsk gulfs in the southeastern part of the Caspian Sea. It belongs to the *peremjot* type, since the float lines of the hooks are tied to a common line. Seal cracklings or small live fish serve as bait. Used exclusively for the capture of huso, these hooks are dropped to a depth of 8-120 sagenes (16-257 m.) in the inlets or the deeper parts of the sea.

30. Kusnetzow (1898), p. 27.

31. Jankó (1900), II, 507, Figs. 481 and 482.

32. *Ibid.*, p. 507, Fig. 484, and p. 508, Fig. 488.

33. Шульц (1861), pp. 45 and 138. It is perhaps this huso fishing tool which the report of a former illustrated weekly in Budapest describes—unfortunately without sufficient details (cf. Asztrakán [1858]).

The haul so made consists largely of sterile old huso (хлопуня),[34] known as giants even among the great huso.[35]

3. GEOGRAPHICAL DISTRIBUTION OF SAMOLOVS IN RUSSIA

Herman and Jankó were both mistaken in their supposition that the Magyars had become acquainted with the huso hook of the samolov type during their stay in the Volga Valley. On the other hand, Herman was right in establishing the identity of the Danubian huso hook with that used in the Volga, while Jankó's further research into the origin and distribution of the samolov has yielded rich scientific results.

Jankó writes:

Above all, we are interested in the origin of the tool, and our search has to start in the Volga region. The center whence the samolov began to spread was the Volga River itself, and it was from there that Russian fisherman carried it northward, although samolovs could not take root in northern European Russian fishery until sterlet fishing had become popular in the Dvina River; it was likewise from the Volga that the tool spread up the Kama and across the Ural to the Irtysh-Ob Valley, where it is very popular among the Russians and Tatars. Irtysh samolovs are especially interesting; they are of different sizes, usually delicate and thin, sharply pointed, and frequently unbarbed.[36]

Jankó's theory about the samolov's Volga origin is based on the study of much material, and his sources substantiate his conclusions.[37]

Jankó does not speak of the Russian affluents of the Black Sea, where the existence or nonexistence of samolovs is significant from a Central European point of view because these rivers belong to a system connected with the Danube. Let us first remember the Dnieper, a river near the Danube, where samolovs, though not in general use, are employed to such an extent as to have induced the Russian authorities to restrict and even prohibit them.[38]

Evarnickij mentions the samolov among the most important fishing tools on the Dnieper, where it was used to catch huso and other large sturgeon though small varieties of Acipenserideae were caught with nets.[39] This information has a double significance. It shows that the samolov type of hook had an importance here in historical times greater than at the end of the last century, because the size of Acipenseridae in the Dnieper used to be much larger than it has been in recent times. It also shows that while huso samolovs (балберочная снасть) were well known along the Dnieper at the end of the

---

34. Шульц [1861], p. 43.

35. Relying on historical sources, Sabaneev mentions (Сабанеев [1892], II, 518) a sterile huso weighing 250 poods (4,100 kg.), which must have been a huge specimen, considering that the old huso described by Strahlenberg weighed about 2,000 kg. and was 8 sažen (17 m.) long.

36. Jankó (1900), II, 521–22.

37. For bibliographical reference in connection with the quoted text see Jankó's book.

38. Данилевскнй (1871), p. 253.

39. Эварницкий (1892), pp. 474 and 475.

last century, sterlet samolovs (шашковая снасть) were still unknown. The fact that sterlet hooks were already employed at that time on the Volga shows that they must have spread from east to west.

The use of samolovs provided with floats was much more popular on the Don, where they were called "rolling *peremjot*" (накатный перемёт).[40] (This "rolling" nature of the samolov is also emphasized by its Chinese name, "rolling hook"; see Fig. 68.) How much this tool was coveted is strikingly illustrated by strife that broke out between Cossacks and other fishermen because each party regarded itself as having the exclusive right to use it around the estuary of the Don. It seems that the samolov constituted the chief fishing tool of the non-Cossack population. That hauls had become less abundant also in the Don during the second half of the last century was ascribed by the Cossacks to the use of floated samolovs. They thought that samolovs facilitated the work of "foreign" immigrant elements and that this tool could more easily be hidden from the inspectors.[41] The hostility of Cossacks manifested itself also in decrees that prohibited the sale and use of samolovs.[42]

There is, moreover, information according to which samolovs were also employed in the southeastern corner of the Black Sea, on the Rion River near the Turkish frontier, where they were in exclusive use about 1870.[43]

Sources as to the samolov's distribution in northern Russia are much scantier. Jankó refers to their use in the river system of the Ob and in the Dvina River. He cites a remark of Šul'c almost verbatim, according to which samolovs are comparatively new in the Dvina, having been adopted only after the spread of sterlets.[44] Danilevskij confirms that sterlets came from the Kama River to the Vičegda through the North Yekaterin Canal, and from there found access to the water system of the Dvina.[45] The oldest inhabitants of Arkhangelsk say that the first sterlet in the Dvina was caught in the middle of the twenties of the last century, above Holmogor. A peasant caught it in the Suhona with a harpoon, while subsequent sterlet fishers used nets. A fisherman from the Kama taught them at last how to manipulate samolovs.[46] Sturgeons ascend as far as the Dvina, although their appearance is not frequent there.

Further information supplements Jankó's data, Manninen reports that samolovs are known along the Pechora River and its tributary, the Ižma, where the Zyrians use them for sterlet fishing.[47] This information is not without interest, since we know from another source that Acipenseridae of the Pechora include the sturgeon, which are said to arrive there from the Ob.[48] If this

40. Сабанеев (1892), II, 558.
41. Данилевский (1871), p. 148.
42. *Ibid.*, p. 166.
43. *Ibid.*, p. 296.
44. Шульц (1863), p. 12.
45. Данилевский (1862), p. 15.
46. *Ibid.*, p. 49.
47. Manninen (1932), p. 273.
48. Данилевский (1862), p. 71.

is so, it can be taken for granted that samolovs are employed there in sturgeon fishery also.

Jankó advances the theory that the samolov is of Turko-Tataric origin and that only its dissemination is due to Russian fishermen. It should be emphasized once more that such a conclusion was unavoidable on the strength of evidence possessed by Jankó. Even those sources which were not utilized by him substantiate the supposition that Russian fishermen borrowed the samolov from their Turko-Tataric fellows on the shores of the Black Sea. Let us further remember the Turko-Tataric word *carmac*, which designates the samolov of the lower Danube, and let us refer to Danilevskij's description, mentioned above, according to which this tool is used by "foreigners" along the Don. By "foreigners" he surely means the Turko-Tatars, as distinguished from the autochthonous Cossacks (considered nowadays to be 100 percent Russians), who do not use the samolov any more. We must remember that Astrakhan, where unparalleled numbers of samolovs have always been and are still used, has belonged to Russia only since 1554. During the seasonal run of the sturgeon, the city's population is swelled by fishermen, among the Russians are in a minority in proportion to the Turko-Tatars.[49]

Jankó affirms that Finno-Ugrian peoples do not employ samolovs, since he has never seen this tool in the hands of Ostyak but only in those of Turko-Tataric and Russian fishermen in the Irtysh-Ob Valley, although samolovs are widely used in that region. We must agree with him in this respect, since there is but a single source according to which Zyrians employ samolovs on the Pechora River.[50] If this is so, they must have adopted them not earlier than in the last century, at the time of the sterlet's diffusion.

In spite of all these historical analogies (discussed in connection with the description of Danubian samolovs), as well as more remote analogies to be discussed in subsequent chapters, Jankó's theory seems doubtful. He claimed that samolovs first appeared during the Völkerwanderung, but it is probable that this fishing tool was already well known at that time at many points of Eurasia situated along the rivers in which the great seasonal runs of the Acipenseridae occurred. As for his other claim—that samolovs appeared on the Volga—it is more likely that they are of northern origin. This theory as supported by the existence of Lapp samolovs of the Viking period, discussed later in this monograph.

4. THE MORPHOLOGY OF RUSSIAN SAMOLOVS

The anchor-shaped huso hooks of southern Russia have already been discussed in connection with the similarly shaped Danubian huso hooks. Since additional data in this respect is lacking, a morphological analysis of the one-

49. Moynet (1867), p. 81.
50. Manninen (1932), p. 273.

branched type will have to suffice. In this analysis, sturgeon hooks of the Volga must be distinguished from those of the Ob.

The only sources for the formal investigation of samolovs used on the Volga (more correctly, samolovs used in the river system of the Volga) are the few illustrations that are presented in the report of the Baer-Danilevskij expedition. These illustrations are, unfortunately, so conventional (as a matter of fact, they are merely simple industrial drawings) that not much can be learned from them. All the hooks appear to be smoothly polished factory products made for Russian industrial fishing establishments. On the other hand, it is evident that the small private fishermen of the rivers of southern Russia must have used hooks of forged iron that were different from industrial products both technically and morphologically.

Since the origin of the Danubian huso hooks can be taken for granted as of southern Russia, they may serve as a secondary source for the analysis of the ancient form of Volga samolovs.

Šul'c, the author of the report on the Baer-Danilevskij expedition, depicts two types of huso hooks: one from the Caspian Sea (Pl. XIV, No. 1) and another from the Volga (Pl. XIV, No. 2).[51] Both are of the recent variety, floatless and hanging down from a line. The unflattened ending of the shank and the fact that the hardly perceptible barb is made with a chisel point shows that they were produced from commercial wire in factories. All other Caspian Sea and Volga samolovs represented in the album are smaller and were used for sterlets. The length of the hooks is between 8 and 10 centimeters. There is one among them (Fig. 43)[52] whose shape is faintly suggestive of the traditional form as seen in old forged hooks. This seems to be closest to the Danubian huso hook. The section of the shank is square, and the point shows an unusual form. We may assume that the drawing in question represents a forged object of popular origin and that it is only the rigidity of the industrially conventional representation that imparts a schematic character to it.

The album contains pictures of many sterlet hooks, all of which seem to be serially manufactured industrial products. They are made of cylindrical wire, and their barb shows the customary conventional curve characteristic of factory products.

The history of fishermen's migrations justifies mentioning the sterlet samolovs of the Dvina Valley side by side with samolovs of the Volga. A specimen is represented in Plate XIV, No. 3.[53]

Hooks used in the Ob Valley display a special morphological feature in that the bend turns with two breaks toward the crook. A forged-iron hook, shown by O. Herman (Fig. 44) in one of his note books, seems to be the earliest specimen. Herman saw it in the Russian pavilion at the Paris Exhibition of 1900

51. Шульц (1861), Рисунки . . ., Pl. A IV.a 1 and 2.
52. *Ibid.*, Pl. A IV.a 3, Fig. 6.
53. Шульц (1863), Рисунки . . ., Pl. A IV.a 4, Fig. 2.

and as explanation wrote on his picture: "Huso-hook. Siberia."[54] Presumably it originated in the Ob or the Yenisei region. Thus it is not exactly a huso hook but one used for sturgeon in general, its size (about 16 cm) agreeing with that of Danubian huso hooks. Its shank is tapered, and, since hooks made of industrially manufactured pieces of wire have uniformly thick shanks,

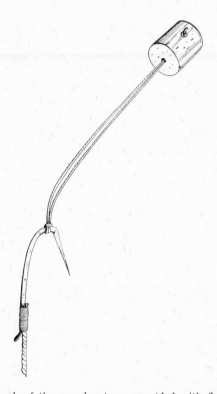

FIGURE 43.—Sterlet hook of the samolov type, provided with float. Volga. (After Šul'c.)

it is undoubtedly a forged hook. The circularly twisted ending of the shank also reveals that the hook in question is no factory product.

Varpakhovskij[55] presents a beautiful series of hooks from the Ob. The largest one in the series is 11 cm., and it is used in the bay into which the river empties (Pl. XV, No. 1). The next two hooks serve for catching sturgeon in summer on the Irtysh (Pl. XV, Nos. 2 and 3). Another type of hook is used there for *jurovoj* (юровой) fishing under the ice in winter (Pl. XV, No. 4). The series also includes a summer sturgeon hook from the Tobol (Pl. XV, No. 5), a summer sterlet hook from the Irtysh (Pl. XV, No. 6), and a sterlet hook for winter *jurovoj* fishing, also from the Irtysh (Pl. XV, No. 7). The reproductions in Plate XV are not of photographs but of carefully executed drawings. It is unfortunately impossible to tell which of the hooks are hammered and which are factory made. The large hook from the Bay of the Ob is barbed, the shape of the barb betraying its industrial origin. The others are unbarbed, have an exceedingly narrow crook and a very sharp point, and may, therefore, have been made in private workshops. It can be seen from the pictures that the winter *jurovoj* hooks are smaller than the summer tools.

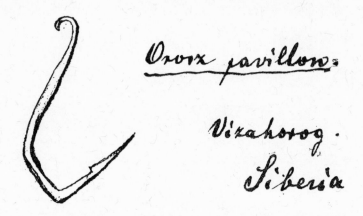

FIGURE 44.—Sturgeon hook of the samolove type. Ob or Yenisei, Siberia. (Herman's sketch in the Russian pavilion at the Paris World Exhibition of 1900.)

FIGURE 45.—Norwegian hook, similar to the sturgeon samolov used on the Ob. Bergen, Norway. (On the evidence of Buch's description, after Herman's drawing.)

A hook in the collection of the Budapest Ethnographical Museum (Pl. XV, No. 8) shows the same features as Herman's drawing and the hooks of Var-pakhovskij.[56] It was acquired by Jankó along the middle Ob, and he makes reference to it in his book.[57] It is similar to Type VII of the Danubian huso hooks but, having been made for smaller sturgeon, is correspondingly reduced in size.

56. Inventory No. of the Budapest Ethnographical Museum: 40.091.
57. Jankó (1900), II, 521.

L. Buch described a morphological counterpart of the Ob hooks in his Norwegian travel book at the beginning of the nineteenth century. He says that the hook, presumably used for codfish, is a characteristically Norwegian type made by the smiths at Bergen. The shank and the crook form an angle of 45 degrees. The shank is straight when the hook leaves the workshop, and only after it has been purchased does the fisherman give it a bend, sometimes at a higher, sometimes at a lower, point. When this has been done, he attaches the hook to the line.[58] Following Buch's description, Herman made a drawing illustrating this process (Fig. 45).[59] It is probable that later the smiths gave the hook its definite shape in their workshops so that the fishermen were spared this extra work.

58. Buch (1870), pp. 307–8.
59. Herman (1893), p. 383.

CHAPTER V

ARCTIC HOOKS

I. LAPPIC SAMOLOVS OF THE VIKING PERIOD

IT HAS BEEN noted that Herman was the first to discover the analogy between Danubian huso hooks and Volga samolovs, and this discovery is important in tracing the history of this tool to more remote times.

In the course of his ornithological investigations in Scandinavia Herman tried to find traces that might lead to information about the manner of fishing in the "original home" of the Finno-Ugrian peoples. Although his Norwegian journey served ornithological purposes in the first instance, the author of the *Book of Hungarian Fishery* did not abandon the work he had begun. He said: "Who knows? One might discover some tool analogies in the Far North, among the Lapps, who are regarded as belonging to the Finno-Ugrian race. I discussed the subject very vividly with Virchow [one of the greatest ethnologists of the age] during my stay in Berlin."[1] Herman devotes a separate chapter of his travel notes to the description of Laplandic fishing methods and takes special notice of the "beautiful prehistoric hooks" from the Varanger Fiord kept in the Museum of Tromsø. Comparing them with recent types, he shows the picture of one of these hooks as the archetype of modern fishhooks (Fig. 46).[2] The analogy is not quite convincing because Herman also presents in his picture the front view of an English kirbyhook, although it is essentially different from the ancient Lappic hook.

The fossil hook shown by Herman is made of reindeer horn, and its barb is very slender. There is no knob or fluting for the attachment of the line at the end of the shank, so the hook seems to be incomplete. The hook continues at the bend with a broad and flat appendix, pierced by a round hole.

Fifteen years after Herman's publication Solberg wrote an essay on a similar type of reindeer huso hook pierced at the bend. The hooks he described were found in the Island Kjelmø (formerly Kjelmesø), which lies in the Varanger Fiord (Norwegian Lapland). Presumably the hook described by Herman also derived from this island. Solberg's description refers to nine hooks pierced at their bend (Pl. XVI, Nos. 1-9),[3] and there is but one among them on which a slightly protruding barb is perceptible (as seen in Herman's drawing). All the others are plain hooks with smoothly polished crooks. The latter are slightly

1. Herman (1893), p. 377.
2. *Ibid.*, p. 384.
3. Solberg (1909), p. 29, Figs. 2–4, and p. 30, Figs. 5–10.

turned outward and have a very sharp point. In thus hooks there is a small knob at the end of the shank, while in the rest the end of the shank is fluted. It follows that the line was attached to the first two hooks by means of a loop,[4] whereas the rest were similar to the usual sturgeon hooks insofar as the line was fastened to the end of the shank by being wound in dense coils. Since, regrettably, Herman's report is unknown in the international literature, it is Solberg's later publication that is quoted when reference is made to this type of hook.

FIGURE 46.—Lappic reindeer-horn hook from the Viking period. Varanger Fiord, Norway. (In the Museum of Tromsø, after Herman.)

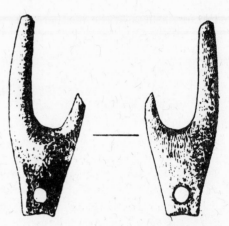

FIGURE 47.—Fragment of Lappic hook from the Viking period. Yekaterinin Island, Murmansk Coast. (After Gurina.) Length, 4,7 cm.

Knowledge of this type is further enriched by Gurina,[5] who presents the torso of a hook from Yekaterinin Island (Kola Bay) that is similar to Solberg's hooks from Kjelmø (Fig. 47). The island is situated on the northern side of the Kola Peninsula on the Murmansk Coast, east of the Varanger Fiord. Both point and shank of the hook are missing, but it is easy to reconstruct it on the analogy of the Kjelmø hooks. Although mangled, the hook shows its most characteristic feature—the hole pierced through the broad plate below the bend. Only this single piece was unearthed there, and Gurina attributes this poor result to the fact that excavations on a much larger scale were in progress on the island.

Not only this remnant of a hook but also the ceramic material unearthed in Yekaterinin is similar to that found on Kjelmø Island, so all these finds seem to be the relics of a common culture.[6] Gurina regards his find as of neolithic type from the early Iron Age and dates it from the second half of the

4. Hook shanks ending in a knob were already widespread in the Neolithic Age. The line may have been fastened to it in the same way as is done nowadays (cf. Seligo [1926], p. 47, Fig. 36; Ghelase [1951], etc.).

5. Гурина (1953), p. 382, Fig. 25, No. 2.

6. *Ibid.*, p. 386.

first millennium B.C.[7] Solberg dates his finds from the last period of the "arctic stone age," which was characterized by the occasional use of iron.[8] This would, probably mean a time between the birth of Christ and the eighth century A.D.[9] Shetelig seems to settle the problem by suggesting that the hooks in question represent that northern "epipaleolithic culture" or "bone age" that is based on western European paleolithic traditions.[10] The objects excavated in the Lappic colonies belong to the Viking period ninth to eleventh centuries A.D.[11] Shetelig's chronological determination and his reference to Laplandic provenance confirm Sirelius' claim that these hooks were used by the forefathers of the northern Lapps.[12]

Paleoarcheologists have, so far, failed to explain the precise use of these curiously shaped hooks. Solberg thinks that the hole at the bend served for the attachment of the bait. He writes in his essay that, faced with these fossil tools, the oldest inhabitants of the region seemed to remember from their youth a kind of faintly similar hook made of reindeer horn and the wood of the juniper tree. They said these had been used by fishermen in the interior of Finmark (Northern Norway) and also in Finnish Lapland, especially in the area of the Kautokeino and the upper Torneå rivers. The hooks they remembered had a similar hole for the attachment of bait. Solberg remarks that he has never encountered similar modern hooks.[13] So far as is known, no report published since that time has mentioned similarly shaped recent hooks.

It may he supposed that the old Laplanders mentioned by Solberg remembered those composite hooks which, though really suggestive of the Viking hooks at issue (Pl. XVII, Nos. 5-9), had no hole at the bend—nor could they have had one, since their coaptation would have become constructionally impossible.

Gurina shares the view that the hole piercing the flat appendix at the bend served for the attachment of bait.[14] Solberg suggests that it was used for cod fishing,[15] and Gurina accepts this theory, noting that Kola Bay abounds in codfish.[16]

All this is, however, nothing but guesswork. To ascertain the truth, the principle of "catchiness" (effectiveness) so often quoted by Herman must be considered. If the Lappic fisherman of the Viking period had fastened the bait to the hole at the bend of the hook, it would have been too far from the point of the crook to catch fish except with the greatest of luck. Knowledge of the hooks and fishing methods of northern Europe justifies regarding these

7. *Ibid.*, p. 388.
8. Solberg (1909), p. 4.
9. *Ibid.*, p. 123.
10. Shetelig (1926), p. 36.
11. *Ibid.*, p. 40.
12. Sirelius (1906), p. 136.
13. Solberg (1909), p. 30.
14. Гурина (1953), p. 381.
15. Solberg (1909), p. 29.
16. Гурина (1953), p. 383.

artic hooks as the archetype of all hooks of the samolov type because of their structure. The hole at the bend of the hook must have served for the attachment of the short float line.

Bone hooks with floats were used singly and not in series, else whole groups of fossil hooks would have been unearthed instead of solitary pieces. Gurina thinks that prehistoric fishermen ceased to use these bone hooks when they became familiar with iron hooks.[17] That the ancient bone hooks were used singly and not serially is further substantiated by the fact that the use of whole rows of hooks is a comparatively recent development; let us remember that anchor-shaped single huso hooks are still occasionally employed in the delta of the Danube. We cannot accept Clark's assertion that rows of serially arranged hooks were known as early as prehistoric times. He bases his assertion on a rock engraving found in the parish of Ytterøy (northern Trondelag) at Kvernevika. This rock engraving shows a dozen halibuts arranged arcwise all of which (save one) are turned head outward. He adds that equipment consisting of several hundred and even a thousand hooks were a later development and came into use when the transport of fish to large and sometimes distant markets had begun.[18] According to Russian research work based on more recent documents, single hooks were exclusively used until the seventeenth century even in northern Norway, where fishery had reached a comparatively high level. Serially arranged hooks, known as ярус in northern Russia, do not seem to have appeared there until the beginning of the seventeenth century, for they were prohibited in Nordland in 1627 for the first time. Repeated several times, this absolute prohibition lasted through the entire seventeenth and the first half of the eighteenth century; it was proclaimed in 1753 for the last time. The serial arrangement of hooks became so popular in spite of official measures that prohibition had lost its effect and was definitely withdrawn in 1763.[19]

As regards the class of fish for which the hooks were used, their samolov type points to Acipenseridae or some other great unscaled fish with sturgeon-like properties. The common sturgeon (*Acipenser sturio*) being indigenous along the northern Scandinavian shores of the North Sea,[20] the provenience of both Solberg's and Gurina's hooks falls within the sturgeon area. Considering geographical factors, it would seem that both sites in Lapland lie at points eminently suited for sturgeon fishing.

Three rivers flow into the Varanger Fiord and two into the Kola Bay. They abound in water, since all of them drain whole lake systems. The mouths of large rivers are especially favorable for sturgeon fishery, as has been noted in connection with the Danube, Don, and Volga. Shoals of spawning sturgeon arriving from the sea can best be caught at the mouth of large rivers. Nowhere along the Murmansk littoral can we find places more appropriate to catch

17. *Ibid.*, p. 387.
18. Clark (1952). p. 89.
19. Данилевский (1862), p. 201.
20. Berg (1932), p. 110.

the masses of sturgeon ascending the river from the arctic sea than the immediate neighborhood of Kjelmø and Yekaterinin islands.

However, excavations produced not only V-shaped plain hooks but also
⌣-shaped barbed ones in both places (the latter type to be discussed later).
The simultaneous occurrence of both types points to a corresponding duality
in the manner of fishing. The ⌣-shaped barbed and baited hooks could
be used for sturgeon as well as any other kind of fish that snaps at food
with its mouth. They may have served for cod fishing; this fish emerges
in large shoals from the depths of the Atlantic Ocean in mid-February
and travels toward the shallow waters of the Norwegian littoral to deposit
its roe.

It was, therefore, due to the regularly recurring annual run of the sturgeon
toward the rivers and the migration of the codfish toward the shallow bays
that these two types of hooks developed. The precisely timed annual reap-
pearance of masses of fish must have yielded copious hauls for prehistoric
fishermen, since fish are less wary during the period of spawning than otherwise. Such lack of watchfulness is especially profitable in the case of large,
closed masses. Clark attached great importance to the seasonal run of sturgeon and regarded it as one of the factors that induced the agricultural-
stock breeding peoples of the Neolithic Age to establish colonies at suitable
points.[21]

A morphological analysis of Lappic hooks of the samolov type from the
period of the Völkerwanderung takes us back to times more remote than the
Viking period. Shetelig's suggestion that the hooks being discussed represent
paleolithic traditions has already been noted. It is easy to trace morphological
similarities in the case of those V-shaped hooks which appeared in western
Norway at the end of the Mesolithic Age.[22] Their structure agrees with that of
the Kjelmø hooks: they are equally large, their crook has an equally sharp
point, and it is equally turned slightly outward. They, too, have the broad,
flat appendix at the bend, though it is not yet perforated.

Special reference should be made to that rich mesolithic series which was
reported by Brøgger from the kitchen-midden find *(kjøkkenmødding)* near
Viste. Three of these pieces are shown in Plate XVII, Nos. 1-3.[23] Similar objects
were reported by Giessing.[24] The material brought to the surface in the Baltic
states constitutes a separate group. An especially long (16,5 cm.) specimen
made of bone was excavated in Pomerania, near Reddies in the district of
Rummelsburg (Fig. 48).[25] Likewise near the Baltic Sea, at Fernewerder in the
western part of Havelland (Brandenburg), a similar hook was found that,
according to Krause, may have been made of the shin of a reindeer.[26] Another

21. Clark (1952), p. 56.
22. *Ibid.*, p. 42.
23. Brøgger (1908), Pl. I, Figs. 1, 5, and 6.
24. Gjessing (1945), p. 117, Fig. 23, Nos. 2 and 3.
25. Christensen (1881), p. 95.
26. Krause (1904), pp. 215–16, illustration: Pl. X, Fig. 325.

similar object is the hook dug up between the White Lake and the Vože Lake, which Russian scientists regard as belonging to the Kargopol culture.[27]

The hooks under review occur, therefore, in two separate groups; one covers the area of the western Norwegian culture, the other that of the Baltic. Shetelig[28] emphasizes the parallelism of and points to contacts between these cultures.

Although the bone hook (Fig. 49)[29] unearthed at Long Island is genetically surely related to the hooks under review, it is not so easy to find the geographical connection in this case. One would have to postulate an arctic path of dissemination like that mentioned for Type III of drilled Danubian hooks.

A veritably insoluble problem is presented by the bone hook in the collection of the Budapest Ethnographical Museum that derives from Tami Island in New Guinea (Pl. XVIII, No. 4).[30] It is not desired to advance a new theory based on undeniable similarity, but the morphological features of this fossil hook impose the idea of an analogy in spite of the enormous distance that separates its site from that of the objects described above.[31]

A survey of the hooks enumerated above will reveal the fact that they have the same broad and flat appendix at the bend as is seen in Lappic hooks of the samolov type. It follows that the Laplandian fishermen were not the first to apply a broad and flat surface to their hooks in order to be able to pierce a hole; such surfaces existed on the much earlier V-shaped hooks as well and offered a good site for making a hole.

One must ask why prehistoric fishermen carved such an unnecessarily large, flat surface at the bend of their bone hooks since not even considerations of a greater stability could have prompted them to do so. An examination of the composite hooks consisting of two members that are still in use among the northern Finno-Ugrians and also among certain primitive peoples will enlighten us in this respect. Plate XVII (Nos. 5-9) shows Pälsi's series of Finnish hooks,[32] and Figure 50 is a reproduction of one such hook pictured by Jankó.[33] Reference to the publications of Manninen[34] and Sirelius,[35] brings to light the same feature in hooks of the Voguls, Ostyaks, and Ostyak-Samoyeds.[36] As a sample of Ostyak hooks, one that was found by Anell[37]

27. Брусов (1952), p. 116.

28. Shetelig (1926), p. 36.

29. Rau (1884), p. 126, illustration: p. 127, Fig. 189.

30. Inventory No. of the Budapest Ethnographical Museum: 64.411.

31. Since the time of Bastian's ethnological school, Leroi-Gourhan, among the representatives of the modern trends, has perhaps most strikingly treated of this constantly recurring problem (cf. Leroi-Gourhan [1943], p. 14.)

32. Pälsi (1912), p. 200, Figs. 15, 16, 17, 18, and 19.

33. Jankó (1900), II, 507, Fig. 482.

34. Manninen (1934), p. 52, Figs. c and d.

35. Sirelius (1906), I, 91, Pl. 207, Figs. d–k; (1934), Pl. 42, Fig. 178; Pl. 43, Figs. 179, 180, and 181.

36. Sirelius (1934), p. 99.

37. Anell (1955), p. 199, Fig. 21, No. 3.

is shown (Fig. 51). This hook was used by Ostyak fishermen along the Kazim River and was composed of wood (shank) and reindeer horn (crook), while fibers of Siberian stone pine served to tie them together.

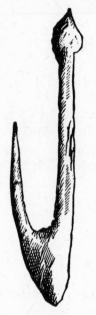  

FIGURE 48.—Bone hook from the Neolithic. Near Reddies, Pomerania. (After Christensen.)

FIGURE 49.—Prehistoric bone hook. Long Island, North America. (After Rau.) Length, 8,8 cm.

FIGURE 50.—Recent hook composed of wood and bone. Jämijärvi, Finland. (After Jankó.)

These composite hooks also have their analogy in Oceania. There is a striking resemblance between the northern European hooks and one in the collection of the Musée de l'Homme in Paris, originally found on Popoko Island (Solomon Islands) (Pl. XVIII, No. 1).[38] Counterparts were depicted by Beasley, one from Tahiti[39] and the other from New Guinea.[40] These hooks, made of wood and composed of two members, are strikingly similar to but much smaller than the Finnish hooks (Beasley's New Guinean piece is the longest among them: 17.8 cm.). Primitive peoples also prepare such hooks from bone, stone, and shells. A sample is presented in Plate XVIII, No. 2; it is in the Budapest Ethnographical Museum[41] and came from the New Hebrides. Another such object is shown in Plate XVIII, No. 3; it is in the Musée de l'Homme of Paris[42] and came from the Solomon Islands. Other analogies can be found

38. Inventory No. of the Musée de l'Homme, Paris: 38.188.572. Other specimens are kept in the Oceanian collection of the museum.
39. Beasley (1928), Vol. I, Fig. 63.
40. *Ibid.*, Fig. 121.
41. Inventory No. of the Budapest Ethnographical Museum: 72. 121.
42. Inventory No. of the Musée de l'Homme, Paris: 34.188.568.

by the reader in the literature, especially in the standard works of Gruvel[43] Beasley,[44] and Anell.[45]

It is quite evident that the composite wooden hook was the prototype of the composite bone hook. Therefore, whenever prehistoric bone hooks consisting of separate members (Fig. 52).[46] are encountered, it should be recalled that their wooden counterparts must have been used in the mass during the prehistoric "lignic" cultures.

FIGURE 51.—Ostyak hook composed of wood and stag horn. Kazim (tributary of the Ob), East Siberia. (After Anell.) Length, 9 cm.

FIGURE 52.—Composite (bipartite) bone hook. Volosova, Veletma (tributary of the Oka), Government Vladimir, Russia. (After Koudriavtsev.)

It was unavoidable that a broad and long extension should develop at the point at which the two members of the composite wooden (and subsequently bone) hooks were joined. It is this structurally reasonable form that appears in the V-shaped non-composite hooks of the Mesolithic Age, that is, at a time when the original reason for the flat appendix was gone.

It is not a new theory that all forms of composite hooks derive from hooks carved from natural forked wood. Reference may be made in this respect to the objects shown by Pälsi (Pl. XVIII, No. 4)[47] and Jankó (Fig. 53)[48] or to any ethnological work dealing with piscatology.

It is now possible to establish the genealogy of Lappic samolovs as used at

43. Gruvel (1928), p. 98, Fig. 75; p. 99, Fig. 78.
44. Beasley (1928), Pls. 142, 143, and *passim*.
45. Anell (1955), p. 109, Fig. 7, Nos. 6 and 7; p. 155, Fig. 14/b; Plate IV/B, No. 1.
46. E.g., Koudriavtsev (1893), p. 252, Fig. 29, and numerous other publications.
47. Pälsi (1912), p. 200, Fig. 14.
48. Jankó (1900), II, 507, Fig. 480.

the time of the Völkerwanderung (Fig. 54) and, doing so is only extending the genealogy established by Jankó in connection with Finnish hooks.[49] It was amplified by Sirelius,[50] who applied it later to Vogul, Ostyak, and Ostyak-Samoyed hooks.[51]

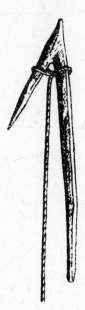

FIGURE 53.—Hook made from a single branch. Finland. (After Jankó.)

2. RECTANGULARLY BENT ARCTIC HOOKS

The second hook from the Ob in Jankó's collection (Pl. XIX, No. 1) is a comparatively small sterlet samolov,[52] which is different not merely from Danubian huso hooks but from any hook found in Central Europe. Buch regards it as typically Russian.[53] Herman depicted it after Buch's description (Fig. 55)[54] and demonstrated its "archetype" from the collection of the Tromsø Museum (Fig. 56).[55]

Herman's judgment was sound regarding the origin of ⏗-shaped hooks. The Lappic hooks of the Viking period were indeed their morphological ancestors. Rectangularly bent hooks and Laplandic samolovs not only agree with respect to their age but were, moreover, both excavated at the same places. Rich material has been found on Kjelmø Island (Pl. XIX. Nos. 2-10),[56]

49. *Ibid.*, pp. 506–10.
50. Sirelius (1906), I, 91.
51. Sirelius (1934), p. 99.
52. Inventory No. of the Budapest Ethnographical Museum: 40.098.
53. Buch (1870), p. 307.
54. Herman (1893), p. 383.
55. *Ibid.*, p. 384.
56. Solberg (1909), Figs. 11–19.

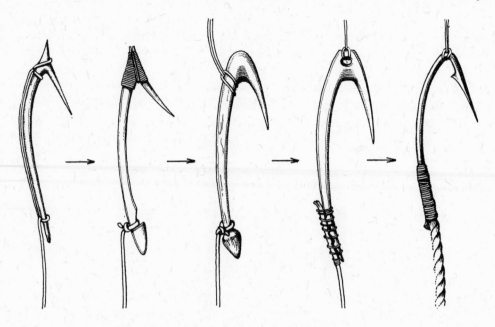

FIGURE 54.—Genealogy of the samolov from the Viking period, archetype of the present iron
samolov with float.

FIGURE 55.—Iron hook, similar to sterlet
hook used on the Ob. Russia. (After Herman's
drawing made according to Buch's description.)

FIGURE 56.—Reindeer-horn hook from the
Viking period. North Norway. (In the
Museum of Tromsø, after Herman.)

while another such object was unearthed by Russian archeologists on Yekaterinin Island (Fig. 57). [57]

The second type of Ob samolov leads once more to the shores of North
America. It has its analogies in the bone hook of the Greenland Eskimos

57. Гурина (1953), p. 382, Fig. 25, No. 1.

(Fig. 58)[58] and in the hooks used at present by Eskimos in Chesterfield Inlet on the northwestern side of Hudson Bay (Fig. 59).[59]

Both the Laplandic fossil variety and a recent North American variety of the ⨆-shaped hooks were made of reindeer horn and provided with barbs. Since the barbs were comparatively large, hooks provided with them seem to have caught the fish by the mouth, so the hooks in question were not of the

FIGURE 57.—Lappic hook made from reindeer horn, from the Viking period. Yekaterinin Island, Murmansk Coast. (After Gurina.)

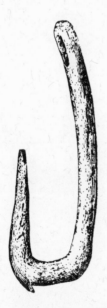
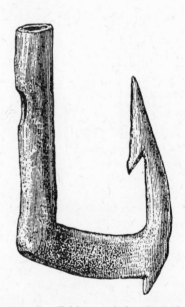

FIGURE 58.—Eskimo bone hook. Greenland. (After Rau.) Length, 14 cm.

FIGURE 59.—Eskimo reindeer-horn hook. Chesterfield Inlet. Hudson Bay. (After Rau.) Length, 5,9 cm.

58. Rau (1884), p. 131, Fig. 200.
59. Ibid., Fig. 201.

samolov type, their barbs argue for a later origin. Clark suggests that barbs were first applied to metal hooks and that it was merely by way of "imitation" that the poor arctic peoples provided their bone and reindeer-horn hooks with a similar device.[60] Although this suggestion sounds strange, it can be proved by data.

All this makes it obvious that ⌐-shaped hooks were originally not of the samolov type. Hooks of this shape, collected by Jankó became suited for sterlet fishery when their large barb had ceased to exist. We seem to be dealing in this instance with the same phenomenon as in the case of the Danubian sterlet hooks at Mohács. We have seen that Central European sterlet hooks have the form of sheatfish hooks and that it was the sharpening of their points that converted them into sturgeon hooks of the samolov type.

60. Clark (1948), p. 65.

CHAPTER VI

HOOKS IN EASTERN ASIA

I. RECENT WOODEN AND IRON HOOKS OF THE SAMOLOV TYPE

Acipenseridae occur in great abundance in eastern Asia. The tributaries of the Amur are particularly rich in sturgeon, and this river system has more or less the same importance in this respect for Asia as has the Volga for Europe. *Huso dauricus*, a giant fish of the Amur, plays the same role in the life of peoples in Asia as does *Huso huso* in Europe.[1]

The fundamental principle of hooks of the samolov type in eastern Asia does not differ from that of the samolovs of Europe and northwestern Asia; the point of the hook catches the fish by getting stuck in some part of its body. The main characteristics of the hook are consequently likewise identical: *(a)* the point is exceedingly sharp and turned outward; *(b)* there is no barb; *(c)* there is, as a rule, no bait; and *(d)* the hooks are afloat with the point directed downward.

Being made of wood, recent eastern Asiatic samolovs need no float. Ancient European samolovs were likewise made of wood, as has been demonstrated in the foregoing chapters in connection with recent Turkomanic huso hooks and Finnish wooden hooks. However, in the case of both European and eastern Asiatic wooden hooks only the shank consisted of wood, while the point was either bone or, lately, metal. The hardness and heaviness of these substances insured the rigidity of the very thin point needed for piercing the sturgeon's thick skin, and pulled the point downward, which was the required position (Fig. 60).

Side by side with such structural similarities, there are significant morphological differences. While European hooks of the samolov type are invariably V-shaped, whatever their age and material, eastern Asiatic samolovs show a characteristic L-shape. Evidence was presented in the preceding chapter that the V-shape of European samolovs was a morphological survival of ancient wooden hooks composed of two members. The same is true of the eastern Asiatic wooden hooks, whose L-shape resulted likewise from the manner in which the two hook members were fastened together.

Considering the material of eastern Asiatic samolovs, hooks with shanks made of wood and pointed crooks made of the tusk of the musk-ox seem

---

1. For the varieties of Acipenseridae and their distribution in eastern Asia see sec. 2 of Chap. I. Cf. also the large handbook of Russian ichthyology (Промысловые. . . [1949]) and Mori's work (1936).

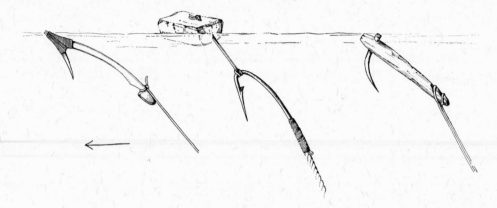

FIGURE 60.—Position in the river of European wood-bone hook, iron hook with float, and eastern Asiatic wood-bone hook, all of the samolov type.

to represent the most ancient type. A hook of this description is reported by Margaritov (Fig. 61); it was used by Orochon fishermen, who caught a large fish called "xoë" ("khojo") in the neighborhood of the Amur River and of the Sea of Japan by means of this tool. [2] Another hook of this class was depicted by Anell (Fig. 62); it was used by Gilyak fishers, who caught a fish

FIGURE 61.—Orochon hook made of wood and muskdeer tusk. River Amur and the region of the Sea of Japan. (After Margaritov.) Length, about 15 cm.

FIGURE 62.—Gilyak hook made of wood and muskdeer tusk. Sakhalin Island. (After Anell.) Length, 21 cm.

2. Маргаритов (1888), Pl. 3, Fig. 6.

called чевица or гой on the shores of Sakhalin Island by means of this tool.[3] The etymology of the names хоё and гой makes it probable that they refer to the same fish.

Of more recent origin is the hook that has a shank of wood and a sharp point of iron. Five such hooks are presented here, all of them collected from Gilyaks living on the banks of the Amur. One is taken from Schrenk (Fig. 63),[4] two are from Annel's book (Figs. 64 and 65),[5] and two were reported by Jakimova (Figs. 66 and 67).[6]

The first, an Orochon hook, is used with a bait, usually a small salmon or a rosefish (краснопёрка). It is suspended from a line 2 arshins (about 1.5 m.) long, which is attached to a stick anchored by means of a stone. Such anchored sticks can be seen at the entrance of all bays whose shores are colinized by Orochons.[7]

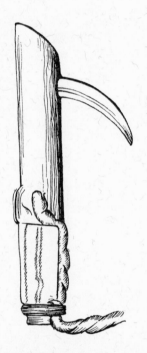

FIGURE 63.—Gilyak huso hook made of wood and iron. Amur. (After Schrenck.) Length, about 38 cm.

FIGURE 64.—Gilyak huso hook made of wood and iron. Village Čil'ma on the Amur. (After Anell.) Length, 34 cm.

3. Anell (1955), p. 199, Fig. 21, No. 2.

4. Schrenck (1881–95), Vol. III, Pl. 41, Fig. 9.

5. Anell (1955), p. 199, Fig. 21, Nos. 1 and 14.

6. B. Anell received the drawings of these hooks from K. A. Jakimova, research worker in the Leningrad Anthropological and Ethnographical Museum. Anell published three of them and gave his kind permission for the other two to be used in this monograph.

7. Маргаритов (1888), p. 19.

It appears from Schrenk's detailed description that only huso and other varieties of sturgeon are caught with this kind of hook. One end of the line is fixed to the bottom of the river by means of an anchor prepared from tree roots and a stone. The hooks are attached to the ends of strings tied to the line. "To the upper end of each hook a thick cord is tied, and a wooden or bark float keeps it on the surface of the water."[8] The wooden shank is thick enough

FIGURE 65.—Gilyak huso hook made of wood and iron. Village Čil'ma, Amur. (After Anell.) Length, 30 cm.

FIGURE 66.—Gilyak huso hook made of wood and iron. Village Čil'ma, Amur. (After Jakimova.) Length, 36 cm.

FIGURE 67.—Gilyak huso hook made of wood and iron. Village Čil'ma, Amur. (After Jakimova.) Length, 33 cm.

to keep the hooks afloat, especially if the whole cordage consists of bark fibers. As a matter of fact, Schrenk's description contains the observation that the principal function of the float is to serve as a signal after the fish has been caught.

No picture of a Chinese huso samolov is available, but ample information about its existence and manner of use is contained in the work of Dabry de Thiersant. He describes 4 to 5-inch strings, bearing one- and two-branched hooks, that are suspended from a thick rope about 200-300 feet long, at intervals of about one foot, so that the whole equipment consists of 200-300 floating hooks. They are unbaited.[9]

An original Chinese representation, as seen in Figure 68, shows the manner in which Chinese samolovs are used.[10] It depicts a scene in which a powerful

8. Schrenck (1881–95), III, 521.
9. Dabry de Thiersant (1872), p. 151.
10. Ibid., Pl. 2, Fig. 1.

fish is captured by the ramifying mass of hooks. They have no bait, are hanging downward, and are provided with large floats. The Chinese inscription on the illustration, "rolling hook," expresses the samolov character of these hooks. The prey is apparently not sturgeon but some other giant unscaled inhabitant of the Far Eeastern rivers. It would prove that hooks of the samolov type are not used merely in sturgeon fishery by Chinese fishermen,[11] although it

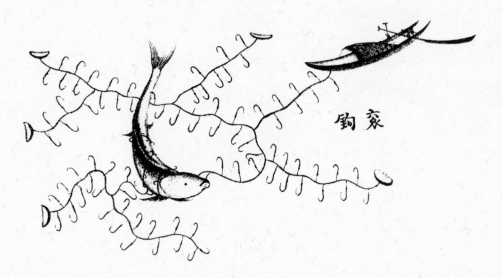

FIGURE 68.—Catching large fish (probably sturgeon) with hooks of the samolov type. China. (After Dabry de Thiersant.) The translation of the Chinese inscription is "rolling hook".

is of course quite possible that the Chinese wood-engraver was not concerned with an accurate representation of the fish. We should remember that, as has already been noted, samolovs serve on Sakhalin Island for other than sturgeon fishing; besides, sheatfish are also caught by samolovs in Russia.

Side by side with these traditional hooks, modern samolovs, prepared from thick iron wire, came to be used at the end of the nineteenth century. They were probably produced in factories. These of course, had to be provided with floats like European samolovs in order to keep them on the surface of the water. A specimen that was employed on the Amur at the end of the last century is presented here from the collection of the Budapest Ethnographical Museum (Pl. XX, No. 1).[12] The wooden float that used to be tied to the hook was still in existence when the Museum acquired the object but disappeared in the disturbances of the war.

The existence of modern iron hooks of the samolov type in eastern Asia is proved by the fact that a certain kind of samolov is called "Japanese *carmac*" (*carmac de Japonia*) in the Danube Delta on the Rumanian seashore.[13] It is

11. *Ibid.*, p. 151.
12. Inventory No. of the Budapest Ethnographical Museum: 81.800.
13. Antipa (1916), pp. 338–39, and Ghelase (1951), p. 148.

floatless so the hooks hang down from the line quite as in the Chinese picture. It is the line itself that is kept on the surface by floats. This tool found its way to the Danube from Astrakhan by the mediation of merchants after 1910.[14] The attribution "Japanese" in the name of the tool was not invented at the lower Danube, since it is also called японка by the Russians.[15] It is quite possible that it really did originate in Japan, which is not so surprising if we remember that the delta of the Volga was very rich in all kinds of fish and attracted fishermen from even quite remote lands. The population is extremely mixed there, including even people from India, who had settled in the middle of the last century.[16] Japanese emigrants, too, may have arrived at Astrakhan and brought their traditional fishing gear to the new colony.[17]

2. ALASKAN FOSSIL BONE HOOKS OF THE SAMOLOV TYPE

Mathiassen, in his report on the North American results of the Thule expedition, describes a fossil hook found at Point Hope in western Alaska (Pl. XX, No. 2).[18] The hook is made of walrus tusk and has a straight shank; the crook juts out at right angles from the end of the shank, continues in a semicircular curve, and terminates in a sharp point.

The shape of the whole hook is a slavish imitation of eastern Asiatic wooden hooks composed of two members. There is a small projection at the juncture of the shank and the crook that looks as if it were a continuation of the latter. This projection has, of course, no function in a bone hook of this type and is just a servile copy of the appendix seen on the original wooden hooks, where it joined the two members of the tool.

The Danish author offers no morphological analysis, nor does he pay attention to the hole at the bend. He surmises that the Eskimos caught salmon with this tool. Yet the hole at the bend signifies that the hook is of the samolov type. It served, as in the case of the fossil Lappic samolovs, for the attachment of the float. The length of the hook is only 3,6 centimeters, considerably less than that of the Laplandian bone hooks, with their lengths of 8-10,5 centimeters. Thus the size of Mathiassen's tool is something like that of the European sterlet hook. It is therefore safe to assume that it was used to fishing for smaller sturgeon, possibly *Acipenser medirostris*, an inhabitant of Alaskan waters.[19]

In the preceding chapter the structural similarity between recent eastern Asiatic and European wooden hooks was pointed out. While structurally similar they were significantly different in shape. The same structural simi-

---

14. Antipa (1916), p. 332.
15. *Ibid.*, p. 358.
16. Moynet (1867), p. 82.
17. In connection with the problem of fishermen's migrations see Sorre (1955), pp. 157–61.
18. Mathiassen (1930), p. 58, illustration: Pl. 14, Fig. 17.
19. Промысловые . . . (1949), pp. 67–68.

larity and morphological dissimilarity seem to exist between fossil European and eastern Asiatic hooks.

The shape of both the fossil Laplandian bone hooks and the fossil Alaskan bone hooks of the Eskimos imitates the form of the composite wooden hooks. Both had a hole at the bend for the attachment of the float.

There are two more fossil bone hooks in the collection of the Thule expedition that reveal genetical relationship with recent eastern Asiatic hooks of the samolov type. They are structurally similar to eastern Asiatic wooden hooks in having their two members fitted together at right angles. One of these objects was found at Point Atkinson, both its shank its and crook are made of reindeer horn.[20] The other was unearthed in the Barter Island; its shank is likewise deer horn, but the crook is made of bone (Pl. XX, No. 3).[21]

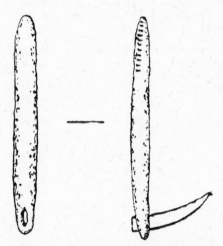

FIGURE 69.—Bone hook composed of two members, from the Neolithic. Angara (affluent of Lake Baikal), southeastern Siberia. (After Okladnikov.)

FIGURE 70.—Bone hook composed of two members, from the Neolithic. Angara (affluent of Lake Baikal), southeastern Siberia. (After Okladnikov.)

Similar fossil hooks, composed of two parts, are reported by Okladnikov from the Angary River, an affluent of Lake Baikal. One of them (fig. 69)[22] has a smooth shank, while the shank of the other (Fig. 70)[23] is grooved for the attachment of the line. Both hooks consist of bone and derive from the Neolithic Age.

An anlogy from northern Europe can also be presented. A hook was excavated at Anholt (Randers amt) in the eastern part of the Jutland Peninsula that is

20. Mathiassen (1930), p. 11, illustration: Pl. 1, Fig. 9.
21. *Ibid.*, p. 24, illustration: Pl. 5, Fig. 13.
22. Окладников (1950), p. 95, Pl. 9.
23. *Ibid.*, p. 91, Pl. 7, No. 15.

regarded by Danish archeologists as belonging to the "Pitware" culture and dated from the middle period of the Neolithic Age (Pl. XXI, No. 1).[24] Its shape is undoubtedly the same as that of the Alaskan fossil samolov discussed earlier in this chapter, and therefore it is related to the L-shaped eastern Asiatic hooks. The small projection on the outside of the bend is certainly a formal relic also in this case, and seems to prove that L-shaped wooden hooks composed of two members must have been known to northern European fishermen of the Neolithic era.

That the fossil hooks from Alaska and Lake Baikal are similar, both morphologically and structurally, to recent hooks from the Amur can be explained by geographical—or, rather, hydrographical—factors. Yet, the analogy of the Jutland hooks is a less easily solvable problem because of the tremendous dinstaces involved.

Except for the fossil bone hook of Alaska, which, as has been noted earlier in this chapter, shows a hole at the bend, none of the other prehistoric hooks showing the Asiatic L-shape can surely be said to have been provided with floats. Therefore, they cannot be termed hooks of the samolov type.

3. OCEANIAN ANALOGIES TO EASTERN ASIATIC HOOKS OF THE SAMOLOV TYPE

The path through which L-shaped composite Asiatic hooks spread leads us to very far regions: hooks that are quite similar to recent samolovs indigenous along the Amur can be seen in New Guinea and New Zealand. Affinity between the two types is perfectly clear in spite of the great distance.

Chapter V, section 1, contained a reference to surprising morphological analogies between certain northern European and Oceanian hooks. Although the existence of similarities was undoubted, the distance between northern Europe and the Pacific Archipelago was too vast to permit of definite conclusions.

The situation is, however, different regarding the relationship between eastern Asiatic and Oceanian hooks. Interethnic influences may well be supposed to have spread through the waterways that connect the Pacific islands and along which migrations of fishing peoples can be proved to have occurred.[25]

Plate XXI, No. 2, shows a representative specimen of the Oceanian hooks in the collection of the Musée de l'Homme, Paris.[26] Its shank is wood and its crook is made of thick seashell. It was used in New Guinea on one of the Admiralty Islands. Hooks of the same type are also encountered in New Zealand; one of them is shown by Beasley[27] and another by Skinner.[28]

24. Glob (1952), p. 131, Fig. 625.
25. Cf. Haddon and Hornel's standard work.
26. Inventory No. of the Musée de l'Homme, Paris: 50.30.491-2.
27. Beasley (1928), Part. 1, Fig. 10.
28. Skinner (1915), Fig. 1.

The Pacific hooks were afloat like other samolovs, so their point was directed downward. Although there are no sturgeon in those regions, the hooks under review were presumably baitless, and the fact that they were intended to catch the prey by getting stuck in its body qualifies these hooks as samolovs.

This assumption is substantiated by Thomazi according to whom most primitive peoples are accustomed to catch fish in the same manner as sturgeon is caught by hooks of the samolov type. He claims that almost all primitive peoples employ rows of serially suspended hooks of the samolov type, especially for fish that have the habit of migrating between two water systems. The hooks hand from long bamboo stems swimming on the surface. In another arrangement a long line, provided with a weight, is sunk to the bottom; the hooks attached to the line are then kept swimming by means of small floats. Thomazi quotes a number of examples, among others the technique employed in certain areas of Senegal in which fishermen pull a long rope across the river on which shorter lines of varying lengths are hung. These lines are from 60 to 100 cm. long and each carries a baitless hook. A whole fence of hooks is thus formed across the water to catch the fish attempting to pass. The trap is set up in the evening and removed in the morning. Thomazi adds that this procedure is the same as that employed on the Volga, where sturgeon is caught with samolovs in an identical manner.[29]

29. Thomazi (1947), p. 98.

CHAPTER VII

LIFE-STORY OF HOOKS OF THE SAMOLOV TYPE

I. MANUFACTURE OF THE TOOL

a) Hook

RUSSIAN DOCUMENTS FROM the eleventh to the sixteenth century make frequent reference to hooksmiths (удник), who produced chiefly fishhooks but also other kinds of iron fishing tools, for example, harpoons and *bagor* (a shafted crook used in sturgeon fishery during the winter season).[1]

That the forging of fishhooks had developed into a special profession proves that the demand by Russian fishermen for hooks was very great in historical times. It seems that fishing with hooks was considerably more popular in Russia than even in the river system of the Danube.

Central European sources contain no references to hooksmiths or harpoonsmiths, nor did we encounter these terms in the course of our field work. Fishhooks are, as a rule, made along the Danube by farriers and especially by gypsy nailsmiths.[2] This is, however, not their chief occupation. There must have existed one or two Hungarian smitheries (on the banks of the Tisza River, in particular) where fishing tools were made. Certain types of harpoons are widespread along the middle portion of the Tisza, and they are unmistakably the products, if not, of the same hand, at least of the same workshop. This applies to a certain type of sheatfishhook also. It seems that certain smiths, aware of the great demand, specialized in the manufacture of fishing tools, which were then sold at various fairs.[3] On the other hand, nothing seems to indicate that smitheries along the middle Danube had engaged in the manufacture of huso hooks. Most such tools were brought to this region by Rumanian boatmen, who transmitted them to the fishermen, and local smiths used them as models.

Having remained a handicraft and retained its peasant-popular character throughout, the manufacture of hooks had reached an unparalleled level in Russia about the middle of the nineteenth century. The inhabitants of the villages Bezvodnyj and Krasnyj Ramenyj on the bank of the lower Volga have

---

1. Колчин (1953/A), p. 143.

2. Cf. also Петровић (1941), p. 76.

3. It was customary throughout Europe in the nineteenth century for hammersmiths to go to fairs to sell their products, e.g., ploughs, harrows, shepherds' hooks, etc., and this custom is still alive in many places.

long been known as former masters of hook-making. Whole families are busy during the winter months with manufacturing fishing tools. Adult men perform the heavier work of forging the iron, making wire, and cutting it into pieces, and young men transform these into crooks and incise barbs of adequate size at a certain distance from the point. They also sharpen the point and flatten the end of the shank for the attachment of the main line. Young girls, as well as married women, after having finished their domestic work, busy themselves with sorting the finished hooks according to size. Hooks of the same size are arranged in groups of one thousand and placed in woven rush sacks on which the weight is indicated. According to whether they are intended for fishing in the open sea, in inlets, or in rivers, the hooks are divided into those with thin and those with thick shanks, so the weights of the individual packages—while each contains a thousand pieces of the same size—are different.

In general, three types are used in open-sea sturgeon fishery. Their respective weights per thousand units are 3 poods (49 kg.), 2 poods 20 funts (41 kg.), and 1 pood 30 funts (29 kg.). Likewise, three types are used in rivers for sturgeon fishery. Their respective weights per thousand hooks are 1 pood 20 funts (25 kg.), 1 pood 10 funts (20 kg.) and 1 pood (16 kg.).

It can be seen that, on account of their size and thickness of shank, sea samolovs are heavier than river hooks. Besides, differences of weigh are greater between the sea hooks than within the category of river samolovs. All these hooks represent a new class in that even the heaviest of them are comparatively light.

The hooks are so bent as to make the length of the crook one-third that of the shank and to make the crook and shank parallel.

During high water in the Volga, that is, in June and July, merchants from the districts of Saratov and Nizhegorod arrive in Astrakhan. Their huge ships and barges are crammed with fishing tackle—thousands of sacks filled with all sorts of hooks and great bundles of cordage and nets. The merchants had ordered the required accessories from the hooksmith in the preceding autumn, and they put these tools in use at the delta of the Volga and on the shores of the Caspian Sea. The annual number of hooks brought to Astrakhan was approximately 11 million at the middle of the last century, a figure unparalleled in Eurasian fishery.[4]

Next in rank to Astrakhan is Rostov, another great market of fishing tools, which satisfies the demands of fishermen from the Don region and even from the littoral of the Azov and Black seas.[5]

The fisherman, after having purchased the necessary quantity of hooks and lines, assemblies his different samolovs. He cuts the string for the side lines into short pieces and attaches them to the main line at adequate intervals. He then charpens the points of the hooks and ties the hooks to the ends of the side lines. The thin string that connects the hook and the end of the side

4. Шульц (1861), pp. 37–39.
5. Данилевский (1871), p. 166.

line (by means of winding) is called рубашка ("shirtlet") by Russian fishermen. It usually becomes frayed by the end of the season. The life span of the hook itself extends over two seasons; it becomes almost totally worn away in two years by repeated filing and sharpening. They say that "a hook wears out two shirts."

The fisherman uses a small delicately ridged file for sharpening the hooks. A measuring rod helps him to give equal length to the strings that connect the hooks with the line. He fits the strings to the rod and cuts off their excess length. He then unthreads the string, places the end of it upon the flattened end of the hook's shank, and fastens it there by a closely coiled thin cord. In order to arrange the hooks at equal distances on the line, the fisherman winds the latter round his hand, and it is at this distance that he attaches the string of the next hook to the line.[6]

Since it is the fisherman himself who assembles his fishing gear, he is in fact, the maker of the tool. It is he who determines the character of any given samolov, since there are different ways of employing one and the same hook—floated or suspended, at this or that height, etc. He determines the length of and the distance between the side lines hanging from the main line. It has been noted that the fishermen of Bergen model their hooks at discretion. The words of an informant from the Tisza River will show the test a hook (in this case, a sheatfish hook) has to undergo before being cast into the water. "A fisherman, before actually putting it to use, will test his hook by attaching it to a nail driven into the corner of the table and pulling it. Soft hooks will stretch, too hard ones will break. Neither is good, since fish can easily escape in either case. Good hooks are sufficiently hard and yet elastic."[7]

Fishermen along the Balkan portion of the Danube and also Russian fishermen attach great importance to having the point of their huso hooks very sharp. Sharpening is performed on small workbenches by means of files. The hooks are kept in position by two wooden forks, each of them fixed to opposite sides of the bench. The fisherman places the hook on an anvil in the middle of the bench and files it or, if it happens to be deformed, hammers it to the correct shape (Pl. XXII, No. 1).[8] Serbian fishermen carefully examine their hooks from their boats at certain intervals and refile those with nicked points.[9]

b) Cordage

The material and dimensions of the main line are determined by local tradition and the variety of sturgeon to be caught. The main line of Danubian huso hooks had the same thickness as that of the large dragnets. Hungarian fishermen used to call the main line of huso hooks *in* ("sinew"), the same term applied to the dragline of nets. The somewhat thinner main line of sterlet hooks was called *zsinór* ("string").

6. Шульц (1861), p. 39.
7. Szabó (1937), p. 379.
8. Antipa (1916), p. 348, Fig. 154.
9. Петровић (1941), p. 79.

The main line of the Volga samolovs and the side lines from which the hooks hang are made by the inhabitants of the villages in the Nizhegorod and Gorbatov districts. Suitable ropes and lines are also twisted from hemp of a good quality in the Šack district of Tambov province and in Saratov itself.[10]

The lines of the archaic wooden huso hooks used by the Gilyaks on the Amur show almost prehistoric features. Both the main line and the thinner side lines from which the hooks are suspended consist of willow fibers.[11]

c) Preservation of cordage

Fishermen on the Volga and the Caspian Sea treat their samolovs with a vegatable substance to prevent their being "eaten" away by salt water and the so-called "sea pest" or "whiteness." The latter is especially dangerous in August, when the "water is flowering," that is, covered by a rustlike dark brown or greyish brown substance that darkens all objects and that reduces new nets to rags in seven days if it comes in contact with them.

As a precaution, fishermen impregnate their tools with the sap of oaks and pines brought to Astrakhan from the upper provinces. Poor fishermen prefer the use of grasses (крутик and узик) instead of expensive tree bark brought from afar. They call the two grasses by the collective name "дубняк" ("oak grass"). It grows in abundance on the shores of the Caspian Sea, on the islands of the Volga, and also along the Ural and Terek rivers. The fishermen collect it in spring, tie it into bundles, and dry it in long rows. Fishermen living on the banks of the Kura River frequently use the bark of pomegranate trees for the preparation of hook lines; such trees grow wild in the Šemakhin province. The samolov lines are placed in huge cauldrons and boiled for six hours in the sap of the oak grass. Frequently, the grass is boiled first and the tool put into the juice afterward. Impregnated in this way, the cordage of samolovs becomes black. Impregnation is followed by the operations of sharpening and tarring.[12]

Huso (and, lately, also sterlet) fishing gear is boiled in tar by Central European fishermen. Fishermen of the Balkan Danube use huge cauldrons for boiling tar and impregnating hooking gear.[13] They impregnate the whole equipment—hook, lines, float—but they protect the polished points of the hooks from being tarred by greasing them with dolphin fat.[14]

This detailed description of the treatment of samolov cordage has seemed necessary in order to show the process to which the black color of Danubian samolovs is due.

Chinese fishermen immerse the hemp ropes of their samolovs in a juice

10. Шульц (1861), p. 39.
11. Schrenck (1881–95), III, 521.
12. Шульц (1861), pp. 42–43.
13. Antipa (1916), p. 346, Fig. 152/h.
14. Ibid., p. 335.

obtained from the bark of a pine tree (*ko-šu*) or in the blood of pigs, and dry them thereafter with steam.[15]

d) Float

The float of samolov hooks is worth special attention. It has already been mentioned that the lung of fattened bovine animals served as the float of huso hooks along the lower Danube in antiquity. Hollow pumpkins *(Cucurbita lagenaria)* were used to keep the anchor-shaped lower Danubian hooks afloat in the eighteenth century, and similar floats are still employed for the sterlet-hooks of Serbian fishermen along the Danube. Let it be mentioned in passing that large bundles of faggot, reed, or bulrush, attached to the main line from which the heavy anchor-shaped huso hooks were serially suspended, used to serve as floats. Zaporozhian Cossacks, fishing in Ukrainian rivers, used to attach bundles of кула (?) to their large hooks.[16]

Huso hooks of the samolov type were kept swimming by means of tra-pezohedral floats made of willow bark (балбера), and the smaller sterlet hooks by means of stopper-shaped floats (шашка). Writing of huso hooks, Gmelin remarks that their float consists of willow bark or the bark of Lom-bardy poplar,[17] while only the latter is mentioned by Šul'c.[18] Again, Antipa refers to poplar bark in general.[19] This shows that the floats of samolovs (and also those of nets) are made of more or less the same material all over Europe. In contradiction to these reports, Volkov affirms that the Ukrainian fishermen of the Danube Delta prepared the float of their huso hooks from the "bark of pine trees." This material reached them from the Carpathians via the Prut River or from Poland via the Dnieper.[20] A more recent form used on the Danube is cork, which, imported by merchants from the south, serves not only as a float for sterlet hooks but often also as a float attached to the upper line of nets.

The floats of Volga samolovs (Pl. XXII, No. 1)[21] are made around Kazan and transported to the Volga from Astrakhan. They have different sizes and are sold in bundles of a thousand pieces each.[22]

Floats are regularly tarred, together with the hooks, to make them last longer.

It should be emphasized once more that floats serve as artificial baits. The float is fastened to the bend of the samolov; this is invariably so in Russia and nearly always so on the Danube. It has already been noted in connection with anchor-shaped huso hooks that the willow float (in the case of huso hooks)

15. Dabry de Thiersant (1872), p. 151.
16. Эварницкий (1892), p. 475.
17. Gmelin (1774–84), II, 212.
18. Шульц (1861), pp. 40 and 140.
19. Antipa (1916), p. 335.
20. Вовк (1899), p. 40.
21. Шульц (1861) Рисунки . . ., Pl. A IV.a 3, Fig. 4.
22. Шульц (1861), p. 46.

and the cork (in the case of sterlet hooks) are drawn over the shank. This method also applies to one-branched hooks. Huso hooks were prepared in this manner, for instance, at Tolna about the turn of the century, and, with a view to making the floats look still more like bait, a goose feather was tied to the bend of the hook (Fig. 71) or was stuck into the float itself, next to the float line (Fig. 72). Moved by the waves or the wind, it baited the great sturgeon.[23]

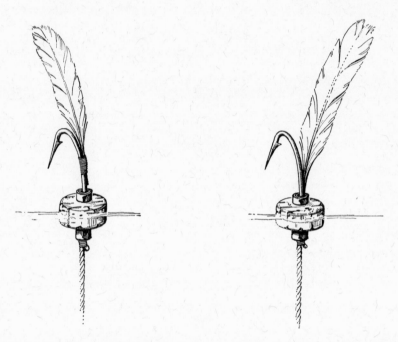

FIGURES 71 AND 72.—Two varieties of huso hooks, provided with feather to attract fish. Tolna, middle Danube.

Floats must have a definite size. Speaking of sterlet hooks, a fisherman from the vicinity of Baja remarked that fishers had to know the velocity of the current and to prepare their floats accordingly. A slow stream requires smaller floats, a rapid stream larger ones; they must be kept afloat but should be weak enough for the fish to "play" with them.[24]

The great variety of floats is well illustrated by the fact that even carefully rounded pieces of ice were employed as floats for samolovs in winter fishery on the Irtysh River.[25]

23. Information received from old fishermen at Tolna.
24. Solymos, manuscript.
25. For a description of fishing under the ice with samolovs see sec. 3 of Chap. VII.

2. THE UTILIZATION OF SERIALLY SUSPENDED
SAMOLOVS IN ICE-FREE WATERS

a) Storing Hooks

When they are not in use the assembled samolovs are usually placed in a series between the branches of bifurcate wooden forks, called by Hungarian fishermen *cserepcsik* (Fig. 73). The ends of the two branches are pressed to-

FIGURE 73.—Bifurcate branch (Hungarian: *cserepcsik*) for the storage of hooks. Widespread in Central and eastern Europe.

gether and so fastened. By this arrangement, the hooks are fixed in a heap and do not injure the hands of the fisherman. Being placed high, the lines hang downward from the hooks so that the chance of their becoming entangled is lessened.

The *cserepcsik*, widespread in the valley of the Danube, serves for the storage of all kinds of hooks. Although data in this respect are lacking, it may safely be assumed that huso hooks have been stored in this manner along the middle Danube for a long time, a manner of storage still in fashion for sterlet hooks. It is, on the other hand, a fact that the *cserepcsik* is used to store huso and sterlet hooks along both the lower Danube (Pl. XXII, No. 3)[26] and the Volga (Pl. XXII, No. 4).[27] This contraption seems to have spread all over Europe; it is known in German-speaking territories,[28] it has been described from Sweden,[29] and it appears even among primitive peoples, where it is made of bamboo.[30]

Wooden forks (called щипчик) to hold the huso hooks were introduced to the Danube Delta from Astrakhan by wandering fishermen in the 1840's.[31]

26. Antipa (1916), p. 349, Fig. 155.
27. Шульц (1861), Рисунки . . ., Pl. A IV.a 4, Fig. 4.
28. Seligo (1926), p. 49, Fig. 39.
29. Hasslöf (1949), p. 35.
30. Gruvel (1928), p. 110.
31. Данилевский (1871), p. 305.

Although the words *cserepcsik* and щипчик seem to be derived from the same etymon, it was not in connection with the tool in question that the word found access to the Hungarian language: it occurs in records dating from 1710 and has, besides, a great number of versions with different meanings.[32]

A special method of packing and transporting samolovs is employed by fishermen of the Irtysh. Samolovs to be used for winter fishery are placed in small wooden tubs, covered with a canvas hood, and closely tied up so as not to get entangled and not to delay the process of unloading.[33]

b) Casting the Hook into the Water

There were several methods of throwing the samolov into the water. Even in quite recent times, fishermen at Mohács often placed their sterlet hooks on the rim of their boats, with the points of the hooks hanging outside the boat, and, while the fisherman rowed, the hook line automatically pulled the hooks to their intended place. A more advanced variant of this method can be observed on the lower Danube. The huso hooks are laid out on a long board, the *"carmac* table," which extends along two-thirds of the boat's length. A square incision at its end serves to fix it to the boat. The rim of the board is provided with an iron plate 7 cm. broad, and the hooks, points downward, are placed thereon. The lines come to lie on the inward portion of the "table," and the hooks slip into the water when the fisherman paddles his boat forward. The slipping of the hooks is facilitated by the weight of the floats (Fig. 74).[34]

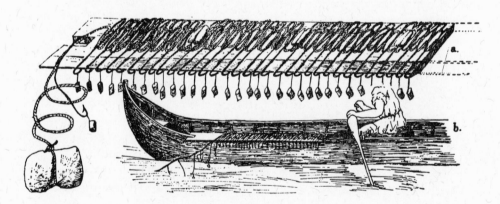

FIGURE 74.—*Carmac* table, board attached to the side of the boat, hooks placed on it slide into the water while the boat is moving. Lower stretch and delta of the Danube. (After Antipa.)

---

32. Generally, it is understood to mean a tool for nipping. Hungarian peasants use the word *cserepcsik* for a certain tool used to castrate animals, while it also means a device used for the compression of hemp, etc.

33. Варпаховский (1898), p. 48.

34. Antipa (1916), p. 331, illustration: p. 333, Figs. 44/a and b.

c) *Fixing the Rows of Hooks in the Water*

Russian fishermen mostly fasten the end of the samolov line to stakes driven into the ground and sometimes to large pieces of stone. Gmelin's picture from the Volga (Pl. XXIII, No. 1)[35] shows a row of samolovs reaching from bank to bank, the main line lying on dry land on both sides. It is tied to a peg and, in addition, fixed by stones on one side of the river, while, on the other, it is tied to a heavy stone. The floats in themselves are unable to keep the whole kit afloat, so separate sticks are fastened to the line to prevent it from sinking, for these are huso samolov hooks, which must remain near the surface.

The line of samolovs used in sea fishery is tied to stakes. These are driven into the bottom by means of long wooden bars and remain there after removal of the fishing tool. A decree forbids fishing with hooks nearer than 7 versts from the shore in the littoral of the Black Sea so as not to hamper the hauling of dragnets by derelict stakes or operative samolovs.[36]

The Russian working method has been adopted by Lipovan fishermen of the Danube Delta. The method, and also the tool necessary for working it, are represented in detail by Volkov. The tool is a log 2-3 m. that broadens out at one end like a bottle. There is a hole at the bottom of the "bottle"; the stake is fitted into it and then pressed into the sand or mud of the river bed from a boat.[37]

In sterlet fishery, the set line has to lie on or near the bottom. Therefore, a stone or other weight is tied to every twentieth hook. One end of the main line is held by an anchor (кошка ["cat"]) or a sack filled with sand. The anchor consists of a few wooden crooks, with stones wedged between the juxtaposed shanks. It looks like the *fentő* (the Hungarian term for the anchor with which hooks are found and lifted) used on the middle Danube. On the Volga the anchor or weight thus fixing the end of the main line is called сторож ("guard"); the Hungarian equivalent of this word signifies objects that indicate the presence of nets or hooks on the middle Danube. Such objects have another name on the Volga. They consist, both on the Danube and on the Volga, of a simple piece of wood, sometimes of reed or some other aquatic plant or a bundle of straw.[38]

The set line (mother rope) of sterlet hooks is anchored by means of a 20-kilogram stone at a distance of 20-30 centimeters from the bank in the Mohács portion of the middle Danube. The stone has to be heavy in order to arrest the motion of the boat when the anchor is moored or inspected in the course of daily supervision. The stone is so placed as not to betray the presence of the fishing gear. The other weights of sterlet hooks are sized and arranged according to the flow of the water. A stone weighing half a kilogram is applied at

---

35. Gmelin (1774–84), Vol. II, Pl. 38.
36. Данилевский (1871), p. 99.
37. Вовк (1899), p. 40.
38. Шульц (1861), p. 46.

intervals of seventh to eighth hooks if the flow is swift, and at suitably larger intervals if it is slow.

The description by Petrović shows that special circumspection is necessary to determine the height at which huso hooks have to be set up in the vicinity of the Iron Gate, where the Danube flows very rapidly.[39] Repeated trials are needed to ascertain the most suitable height of the cross line (and also that of the hooks) above the bottom. A certain height (e.g., 150 cm.) is chosen at the first trial; this is maintained until the result of the first catch is seen. If it is unsatisfactory, the height has to be increased or decreased until the most suitable position is found, that is, the height must be ascertained at which fish are most likely to pass in their migration. If there are several sets of equipment in operation within a circumscribed area, they will be lowered to different depths and subsequently readjusted to the depth of that gear which has given the best results. Around the Iron Gate the usual distance from the bottom is 1,5-2 meters. This is the depth that, according to experience, huso prefer in their upward migration.[40]

d) The Hook's Position in the Water

Since the subject of the hooks position in the water discussed only a summary of what has appeared in scattered parts of this monograph is necessary here.

If the float is attached to the bend of the hook, it will lie in the "classic" position of hooks of the samolov type: it is afloat either on or near the surface and, in any case, above the set line. Anchor-shaped huso or sterlet hooks, and also the recently adopted floatless sturgeon hooks are, on the other hand, generally suspended from the main line and hang downward. Sometimes even these hanging hooks are provided with floats (Fig. 10), which keep them near the surface; otherwise, the weight of the hooks would pull the main line to the bottom.

Since the passage of migrating sturgeon is to be obstructed as much as possible, sometimes a separate hook is tied to each of the floats that hold the main line of the hanging hooks (Fig. 75),[41] or else the hooks tied to the main line are alternately hanging and floating (Fig. 76).[42] This latter variety (*perechi* ["paired"] in Rumanian and двоснасть ["double hook"] in Russian) is mentioned in many eastern European sources, and it is possible that our Chinese picture (Fig. 68) represents such a row of hooks.

It should be noted that hooks may occupy a perpendicular or an oblique position according to the flow of water.

---

39. It has repeatedly been pointed out in this monograph that huso like to swim near the surface of the water. It is only where the stream is very swift that they descend nearer to the bottom, since the current is less sweeping there.

40. Петровић (1941), p. 77.

41. Вовк (1899), p. 41, Fig. 3.

42. Widespread in southern Russia and in the delta of the Danube.

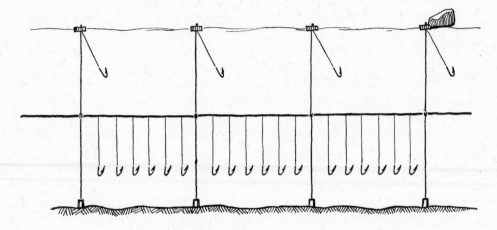

FIGURE 75.—Setting up huso fishing gear by attaching an additional hook to each float from which the main line is suspended. Danube Delta. (After Volkov.)

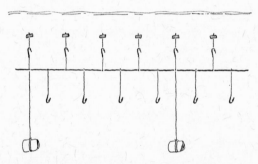

FIGURE 76.—Huso fishing gear in which alternately a hanging and a floating hook is attached to the main line. Widespread in southern Russia and Danube Delta.

e) The Dimension of Hooking Sets and the Number of Hooks

Hooks of the samolov type belonging to a complete set vary in number. Generally speaking, the number of hooks tied to a common line has increased in the course of evolution so that the hooks have come to lie closer to one another, in order to make the barrier of hooks more and more difficult for the passage of fish.

On the Volga River,[43] the usual number of hooks attached to a common line varies between 50 and 100.

On the Rion River, which flows into the Black Sea,[44] a complete set consists of 70 hooks. In the littoral of the Caspian Sea, the set line holds 50 hooks (called dlinnik [длинник]). Two of these sets of 50 make a sčal (счал) and three sets, that is 150 hooks, a peretjaga (перетяга). Finally 150 of these, placed end to end, form a row of about a verst (1067 m.) in length, which thus

43. Шульц (1861), p. 46.
44. Данилевский (1871), p. 296.

contains 22,500 hooks. However, this figure cannot be said to be invariable, since rows may differ as to number of hooks sometimes having as many as 30,000.[45]

A set of samolovs used on the Ob River, consists of 60 hooks, and two sets are usually coupled; the double set is called *svaska* (сваска).[46] A total of 120 hooks per set seems to suffice here, a small number in comparison with the tens of thousands forming a set in the Caspian Sea and the Black Sea. The reader will recall Jankó's statement that Ostyaks do not employ samolovs on the Ob, where only Russians and Tatars catch fish with hooks of this type. Ahlquist tried to explain this phenomenon in the 1880's when he wrote that on the Ob River "large-scale fishery is done only in summer and exclusively by Russians because it needs more enterprising spirit and requires larger capital than that which fate has given the Ostyaks."[47] It is evident from the descriptions of Jankó and Pallas that the chief fishing tools of Ostyaks are the *luma*, a primitive wooden hook, and the harpoon and weir, and it cannot be doubted that samolovs are incomparably more valuable than these archaic tools.

Perimet is the name of the set of 25 hooks used on the Rumanian shores of the Black Sea. Three sets (75 hooks) meak a *tâcam*, *legătura* or *teag* and 160 of these (12,000 hooks) constitute a *zavod*.[48] Units belonging to a common line, tied together by loops, are shown in Figure 77.[49]

FIGURE 77.—Arrangement of main line of huso hooking equipment. Lower Danube. (After Antipa.)

Lipovan fishermen of the Danube Delta also use the *peremet* (переметъ), which consists there of 60 hooks. As a rule, 200-400 and even 600 *peremets* are united into a *carmac* (кармак), which therefore consists of 12,000-36,000 hooks.[50]

Fishing sets on the upper stretches of the Danube do not contain so many hooks, a sign of poorer harvests in these regions. A complete set of the samolov type on the Balkan part of the river consists of 25-100 hooks.[51] Serbian

45. Шульц (1861), p. 40.
46. Варпаховский (1898), p. 45.
47. Ahlquist (1885), p. 211.
48. Ghelase (1951), p. 148.
49. Antipa (1916), p. 328, Fig. 142/d.
50. Вовк (1899), p. 40.
51. Ghelase (1951), p. 148.

fishermen around the Iron Gate tie 15-16 samolovs to the common line, and set up several such sets in a zigzag line behind one another.[52] A row of samolovs, called *szál* ("strand") or *vég* ("roll"), formed by the Hungarian fishermen at Mohács, consists of 50-60 hooks. Four or five such lines are joined together.

The main line of the Chinese set of huso samolovs *(kuen-keou)* is 200-300 feet long and has several ramifications. Hooks are attached to the main line at intervals of a foot by means of strings that are 4-5 inches thick. Chinese huso-catching sets consist, thus, of 200-300 hooks, which are set up in both rivers and lakes.[53]

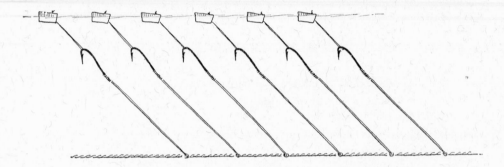

FIGURE 78.—Position of floated hook of the samolov type in swift current.

The hooks occupy a position in the water corresponding to the velocity and direction of the stream. They are perpendicular in the sea and in lakes and are the more at a slaut in rivers the swifter the current is (Fig. 78). According to the law of balance, the heavy and usually curved shank turns downward, while the lighter crook lies above. If the current is swift enough, the crook will lie almost horizontally—it is like a spear turned against the current and swaiting the prey with its sharp point. The float is moved by the stream and attracts the attention of the fish, which begins to lash its tail, thus impaling itself as has already been described in the early part of this monograph). The fishermen of Mohács attach small pieces of cheese to the deep-lying floatless hooks. The sterlet becomes aware of them and knocks its tail against them until it gets itself hooked. This is why the sterlet is invariably gored laterally by the point of the hook. Fishermen tell of a case in which every single hook of a row of samolovs held a sterlet pierced through the tail.

f) Professional Skills in Arranging Hook Rows

Sets of samolovs are used in both unfrozen and frozen waters. Setting them up requires great professional skill, as has been vividly shown by Antipa. The correct placement of samolovs needs considerably greater care than does that of common depth-hooks. The distance of the samolovs from the surface

52. Петровић (1941), p. 77.
53. Dabry de Thiersant (1872), p. 151.

of the water and their direction have to be chosen with regard to the season
and the general condition and temperature of the water.[54] Fishermen setting up their samolovs have to know the most suitable places, be familiar
with the life and habits of the sturgeon, and, moreover, know the bed of the
Danube. They must possess accurate knowledge of the time that sturgeon
assemble at any given point of the river, when the seasonal run begins, and
what course it takes. They must know the places where the fish feed, and
they must be cognizant of the depths at which they are likely to be found at
different seasons. They must know when the fish remain near the bottom and
when they ascend to the surface, where they take refuge when the water
becomes turbid, and which places they frequent when the level of the water
becomes higher or lower.[55] Fishermen know a great deal about nature and its
secrets and are the repositaries of accumulated knowledge transmitted through
a long chain of generations. It is only by possessing a large storehouse of inherited and acquired professional knowledge that they are able to make a
living out of catching the most valuable species of fresh-water fish.

We must first understand that setting up huso samolovs is quite different
from setting up sterlet samolovs. Huso hooks are kept near the surface in
rivers and sunk to some depth in the sea, while sterlet hooks are sunk to the
bottom of rivers. This is because huso prefer moderate depths in the sea but
swim near the surface when ascending the rivers, while sterlet and other
sturgeon like the deeper regions in sea and river alike.

Hungarian fishermen of the middle Danube no longer remember details
of the procedure that used to be employed for setting up huso hooks. On the
other hand, the actual employment of sterlet hooks can still be observed.
Fishermen at Mohács know that when they let their hooks into the water,
they must take an exactly transverse course with their boat, and they are
aware of the fact that the haul is always less satisfactory when they happen
to traverse the Danube in an oblique direction. The Russian documents,
too, note that samolov sets are usually placed across the river (Pl. XXIII,
No. 2),[56] although rows of samolovs installed parallel with the stream occur
as well (Pl. XXIII, No. 3).[57]

The places best suited for sterlet fishery on the Danube are those spots
where the water is comparatively free from vegetable detritus. Where the river
is "littering" (a term employed by Hungarian fishermen), dirt will accumulate
on the sterlet hooks so that their points become incapable of catching the
fish, or else their floats become so overgrown with vegetable matter that
the hooks sink to the bottom. This often happens when the water is very
high, when the flood carries a great deal of coastal rubbish. Places where much
sand is carried by the water are not suited for sterlet fishery, since the sand
buries the stone weight and makes its hoisting difficult. Very soft sand at the

54. Antipa (1916), p. 320.
55. Ibid., p. 335.
56. Щульц (1861), Рисунки . . ., Pl. A IV.a 4, Fig. 1.
57. Ibid., Fig. 2.

bottom is also bad because it retains much rubbish that will then settle on the hook.[58]

g) The Fishing Seasons for the Samolov

The seasonal fishing of huso is very much influenced by the facts that the great sturgeon is easiest to catch during the period of spawning and that female spawners are more frequently captured than are males.[59] The spawning of huso precedes that of all other Acipenseridae.[60] Beginning with Aelianus, a great number of sources affirm that the great sturgeon starts its seasonal migration as soon as the ice sheet of the rivers begins to melt.

Spring is the most propitious season for sturgeon fishing, not solely in rivers but in the open sea as well. Spring fishery starts March 15 and ends May 15 along the Persian shores of the Caspian Sea. About 260 Russian and a few indigenous fishermen participated in it a century ago. The catch made during these two months belonged to the tenant ("host"). When the "official" season was over, fishermen continued to set up their hooks just in order to catch food (котел) for their own meals.[61]

Huso are very strong and are more vigorous in summer than otherwise. During this season, fishermen are endangered and even lose their lives when they haul a great sturgeon ashore. Caught by the hook, the giant fish pulls the boat with great velocity toward the open sea, and occasionally the boat capsizes and sinks.[62] It is noteworthy that the huso remains conspicuously quiet after being caught in any other season of the year, although occasional jerks of the large animal may become troublesome at any time. Lipovan fishermen of the Danube Delta affirm that there is hardly a day on which one of them does not tumble into the water while trying to master a heavier specimen of the great sturgeon.[63]

Springtide is a propitious season for sterlet fishery also, but the fishing gear is put into readiness somewhat later than is the huso samolov because sterlet spawns later than the great sturgeon does. According to information from the region of Baja, sterlet samolovs can be used in "hot spring" and summer, that is, from the middle of April or the beginning of May to mid-October, while the fish is "frisking." "Corked hooks [sterlet hooks provided with floats] are no good when sterlets begin to look for winter quarters."[64]

Chinese sturgeon hooks (kuen-keou) are in permanent service, day and night, from the second to the eighth "moon."[65]

Yield is best if the hooks are set up after storms. Šul'c offers the explanation

58. Information collected by Solymos and the present author.
59. Faltay (1915), p. 107.
60. Данилевский (1860), p. 24.
61. Бэр (1860), p. 119.
62. Сабанеев (1892), pp. 526–27.
63. Arnaud (1936), p. 33.
64. Solymos, manuscript.
65. Dabry de Thiersant (1872), p. 151.

that the rapid flow of the water, whipped up by the storm, sweeps along both large and small sturgeon, and they are unable to avoid the widely ramified mass of hooks. The fish bump against the row of hooks or try to slip through the many lines; striking against a hook, they lash their tails and get caught. As a consequence of their furious jerks, not merely one hook penetrates their skin deeper and deeper but also adjacent hooks get stuck in their body, so that escape is no longer possible.[66]

Šul'c is mistaken if he thinks that any storm is strong enough to whirl along these powerful animals. Hurricanes stir up only the uppermost layer of the water, while the current itself remains practically unchanged. Catching the fish is easier during or immediately after a storm because huso and other sturgeon are frightened by the noise and commotion. Several species are known to become extremely excited by tempests and thunder and to take refuge in some sheltered place. It is said by fishermen at Lake Balaton that at such times sheatfish distractedly dash to and fro. According to a description of Miklós Oláh, archbishop of Esztergom, it was customary in the sixteenth century to frighten the great sturgeon by catapulting big stones into the river, for, disturbed, it became an easy prey.[67] According to Grossinger's report, the richest catch made in the Danube during the whole course of the eighteenth century was that recorded in February, 1723, when a conflagration broke out in the fortress of Buda. The flames reached the ammunition magazine stocked with gunpowder and bullets that had been hidden there by the Turks during their occupancy. The explosion hurled many bombs into the Danube, and the great sturgeon became so perturbed that it was easily caught with nets. Huso, which used to fetch a price of 20-30 florins, per metric ton, was sold for 3 florins on the following day because of the excessive supply.[68]

h) Unhooking the Fish and Hoisting the Hook

According to the length of time that hooks remain in the water, Balkan fishermen of the Danube distinguish two kinds of *carmac*. The first category comprises the "alternating hooks", which are taken from the water, greased, sharpened, and put back every day. The second category consists of the "constant hooks" which, though inspected every day, are removed but once in six or seven days, while the stone weight is always left unmoved.[69]

Alternating hooks of the samolov type do not seem to be used anywhere else. Samolovs are always constant hooks on the Volga; they are inspected twice a day, morning and evening, but are left in place. They are removed from the water once a week to be tarred.[70] Fishermen of Mohács take up their

---

66. Шульц (1861), p. 42.

67. Oláh (1735), cap. XVIII, sec. VII.

68. Grossinger (1794), p. 74. That alarming the fish plays a significant part in sturgeon fishery will be seen in connection with the громка on the Volga as described in sec. 4 of Chap. VII.

69. Antipa (1916), p. 327.

70. Шульц (1861), p. 46.

sterlet hooks once each week (sometimes once each fortnight) for drying and
tarring. They inspect the hooks and take the captured sterlets off every
day. If there are no fish on the hooks for four to five consecutive days, the
whole set is removed from the water and set up again after the lapse of a week.
Some inhabitants of Tolna still recall the times when huso sets were inspected
by a fisherman who, lying flat on his belly at the rear end of the boat, "milked"
the line (i.e., slipped the hook line through his alternating hands).

Petrović offers an instructive description of how huso hook rows are super-
vised in the region of the Iron Gate. Large pumpkins indicate the location of
the samolovs. He fishermen in boats; one of them manipulates the oars so
as to keep his craft near the samolov while another searches for the main
line of the fishing set with the aid of a tridentlike anchor ченгел in Serbian
and fentő in Hungarian). On finding it, he lifts the line from the water and,
grasping it, pulls himself (and the boat) along the whole length of the line.
Coming to a hook, he pulls it from the water, even if no fish is stuck thereon,
and examines its condition. If the hook is unimpaired, he casts it back into
the water. If, however, the point of the hook seems to be blunted, he repairs
it on the spot by means of a tool he carries with him. Jerks of the hook betray
captured fish before he actually arrives at them. Seeing such a twitching hook,
the fisherman approaches it carefully, pulls it to the surface, and tries to
throw one or two of the adjacent hooks on the prey so as to insure the catch.
He then pulls the fish to the side of the boat and with the assistance of another
fisherman hoists it inside either by its gill or by means of another sharp hook.
If necessary, he stuns the fish by a blow on the head.[71]

Shorter reports come from Arnaud,[72] who describes the technique for
lifting captured sturgeon from the water in the delta of the Danube, and from
Schrenk,[73] who describes the process from the Amur. Both these descriptions
(as well as other sources) contain repeated references to two fishing tools that
play an auxiliary part in sturgeon fishery: a short-handled club to stun the
fish, and a strong hafted crook to hoist the captured animal. The hafted
crook used for the removal of the sturgeon from the water is a survival of
presumably the oldest form of huso fishing.

The catch made with hooks of the samolov type does not invariably consist
of sturgeon; it has already been mentioned in connection with Gmelin's description of the huso hook that sometimes scaleless fish are also caught, sheatfish in particular. Hungarian fishermen are unanimous in affirming that
sheatfish are frequently caught with their sterlet hooks. Hooks of the samolov
type are, according to E. Solymos, useful in another respect too; even if scaled
fish do not get stuck, the unusually sharp point may scratch them so that
a few scales will remain on the hook. This, then, gives the fisherman precise
knowledge as to what kinds of fish have passed and when.[74]

71. Петровић (1941), p. 79.
72. Arnaud (1936), p. 33.
73. Schrenck (1881–95), III, 521.
74. Solymos, manuscript.

3. FISHING UNDER THE ICE WITH SAMOLOVS

As the season advances toward winter and the temperature of the water becomes lower, Acipenseridae assembly in holes at the bottom of rivers to pass the cold season in a sort of hibernation. Such holes are called ятов in southern Russia; the deeper they are, the more they are liked by the hibernating fish. Skilled fishermen of the Ural River watch the autumn run of Acipenseridae and note the position of such holes as indicated by the great number of fish that keep swimming above their intended winter quarters. An experienced fisherman will keep his observation secret until the time for fishing.[75]

The ice sheet covering the Volga is pierced by two holes with a diameter of about 2 feet (71 cm.) and with a distance of 2-3 saǯens (4.30-6.40 m.) from one another in a longitudinal direction. A thin string is then tied to the line of the hook, to the other end of which a pole is fastened. The pole is then slipped along under the ice from the first to the second hole. Standing at the hole, the fishermen direct and push the pole in the same way as the so-called "guilding pole" is manipulated in the rivers of the Carpathian Basin. This operation is continued until the entire row of hooks is set in readiness under the ice. Stone weights pull the hook line downward, while it is kept at the desired height with the aid of the *nasluška* (наслушка). A *nasluška* is attached to each *sčal* or *peretjaga*; it serves both as bait and as a signal of a captured fish. Lifting it from time to time, the skilled fisherman can always tell whether one or more of the hooks have caught and, if so, at which point of the *peretjaga*. When he observes that a catch has been made, he unties the guard (сторож)—the long rope fixed to the ice. The tool is now released and can be lifted by means of the *nasluška*. The line is then carefully pulled upward until the fisherman is able to reach the hook on which the great sturgeon is writhing. A blow on the head stuns the animal, and it can easily be lifted to the ice.[76]

A more advanced form of this technique of fishing with samolovs can be observed in the Volga Delta, where huge cross-dykes (учуг) are used. Fishing of this kind is called *gromka* ("noisy"); it likewise is meant to catch different varieties of sturgeon and, as shown by the word, involves a great deal of noise. By making a fearful noise and knocking on the ice sheet, the fishermen try to frighten the fish out of their resting places and drive them onto the hooks or into the nets.[77] The *gromka* will be discussed in detail in connection with samolovs placed before weirs.

A noteworthy technique of fishing under the ice is that employed on the Irtysh River. It is called *jurovoj* (юровой) and is in many respects similar to that winter fishery *bagrenie* (багренье), which—performed with the aid of *bagor* (багор), a hafted crook—is customary among the Ural Cossacks. The word *jurovoj* derives from the groups of fish huddled together in holes

75. Шульц (1861), p. 52.
76. *Ibid.*, p. 42.
77. *Ibid.*, pp. 52 and 125.

for the winter season.[78] Almost all these holes are owned by a peasant or a community, and generally the entire community takes an active part in the process of fishing fixed for a definite day. The day varies according to when ice begins to form on the river, after which an adequate period of cold is needed for the ice to become thick enough for the *jurovoj* to start. While other forms of fishery on the Irtysh last from the second half of November to the last days of December or the first days of January, the duration of *jurovoj* is not more than a few days.

The whole business begins with the "measurement," that is, the distribution of the fishing area among the participants. The area above the hibernal holes, called *jurovaja* (юровая), is staked out and divided into lots (метище or гелешка) according to the number of participants.

The first day is thus devoted to preparatory arrangements, and on the second day the samolovs are set up. The place of the first and the last *metišče* ("lot") of the *jurovaja* is marked. A hole is cut in the ice, and "observation samolovs" are let down through it in order to ascertain whether the fish have been aroused and, if so, to determine whether they have moved up- or downstream. Every participant of the *jurovoj* conveys his tools (samolovs, floats, anchors, balls of twine, poles, etc.) to his *metišče* on small sleds either on the same day or during the following night. Each *metišče* is usually assigned to four or five persons but sometimes to as many as twenty, depending on the distance from the deepest hole with the greatest number of fish.

Hardly any of the fishermen sleep during the third night, that which precedes the beginning of the real fishing operations. It is still dark when they arrive at the river and plant themselves at the *jurovaja*, awaiting the hour fixed for the proceedings to commence. They have to be patient because samolovs must be arranged in daylight so as not to become entangled. Varpakhovskij presents a vivid picture of the fishermen stamping their feet impatiently in expectation of the sign to be given by the *starosta*. Each samolov is attended by at least two persons, who, standing at their *metišče* in utter silence, wait for the report of the *starosta*'s gun. As soon as it is heard, the crowd becomes animated and the whole river begins to ring with the noise of ice-cutting. The ice sheet is soon pierced with holes, at each of which two samolovs are placed. First, a string with an attached piece of carefully rounded ice is let into the water; this serves as a float and is called ледышъ ("icicle"). If the under surface of the ice sheet is uneven, a weight is tied to the float to keep it free from the drift ice adhering to the sheet. The string with the attached float is driven by the current to the lower hole, where it is arrested by a fisherman with the aid of a pole. The end of the pole is sometimes equipped with a small transverse stick, a small board, or some other device to facilitate lifting the string through the hole.

After pulling the string out of the water, the fishermen free it from the ice float and fasten it to the end of the samolov line. This done, they pull the

78. Шульц (1863), p. 108.

samolov back, by means of the string, to the upper hole and anchor the lower end of the string at the lower hole. A piece of stone or frozen earth serves as anchor and must be heavy enough not to be carried away by the current. The anchor itself is tied to its own line, while the end of the string is fastened to a peg driven into the snow beside the hole. The samolov is sometimes only pegged, without being anchored.

As soon as a samolov has been set up, the fishermen begin to cut the other holes. If, for instance, five persons have cut five holes, the first man will set about cutting the sixth hole and after that the eleventh, the second man the seventh and after that the twelfth, and so on.

The object of the *jurovoj* is mostly to catch sterlet. Only three such occasions are arranged on the upper stretches of the Irtysh for sturgeon fishing. Common samolovs are employed everywhere, with smaller hooks for the sterlet and with larger ones for the sturgeon. Sterlet hooks are inspected two hours after being let into the water, while sturgeon hooks are examined more frequently to see whether a capture has been made. The fisherman can always tell by the vibration of the line he is grasping whether there is a fish on the hook.

Samolovs and hooks, when let into the water, rouse the animals resting at the bottom of the river. When one of the samolovs has been hauled out with its prey, the other samolov is automatically let down to the bottom to take the previous samolov's place.

The catch is richest on the first day and very poor during the next three or four days. There are always numerous merchants among the fishermen bustling on the ice, and they buy the fish as soon as they are caught. Some merchants make a blind bargain by "buying samolovs for luck," that is, by paying a lump sum in advance for any number of fish to be caught by a definite hook.

Besides the *jurovoj*, another manner of fishing used to be popular on the Irtysh. It was called на ypa, named after the interjection that served as signal for the beginning of operations, but it has gone out of fashion and had already become very rare at the end of the last century. Each *metišče* was staked out on the area of the *jurovaja* but was not assigned to an individual group of fishermen beforehand. Fishermen, with their sleds and all their tools, assembled on the bank of the river and awaited the signal of the *starosta*. On hearing the report of his gun, each rushed with a tremendous shout "urra" to the lines of *metišče*, those arriving first occupying the best places. Subsequent procedure was the same as in the case of the usual *jurovoj* described above.

Villages lying near the Irtysh are overrun by strangers during winter fishery. Merchants, hucksters, and all sorts of vendors erect stalls and booths where fishermen can spend the money received for their fish. Merrymaking lasts far into the small hours, and often the money anticipated during a whole year is squandered in a single night.[79]

79. Варпаховский (1898), pp. 45–55.

Because of the unreliability of the ice, it is only in the bays of the Black Sea and not on the river or on the sea itself that fishing during the winter season is customary in the delta of the Danube. Attempts at catching fish under the ice have remained fruitless there.[80]

Many forms of winter fishery are known on the middle Danube. All sorts of fish are caught there under the ice, but there are no data about huso or other sturgeon having ever been caught in this area during winter by means of hooks.

4. SERIALLY SUSPENDED HOOKS OF THE SAMOLOV TYPE PLACED BEFORE STURGEON WEIRS

A special Russian way of employing samolovs is to use them as parts of weirs erected across the river. Two varieties are known.

The sturgeon weir, *učug* (учуг), mentioned in Gmelin's travel book, had gates on both sides to allow the passage of ships hauled from the shore, and samolovs were set up across these apertures.[81] Šul'c refers to the *učug* as a relic but confirms the fact that samolovs were formerly used in this auxiliary manner.

Another, much more important, way of using samolovs in connection with weirs is their placement in front of a weir that runs across the whole width of the river. The role of samolov and weir is reversed in this case; the first serves as the primary fishing tool and the second serves only to obstruct the path of the migrating fish which, so hampered, fall victim to the sharp hooks. According to Šul'c, the *učug* and *zabojka* on the Volga, Ural, and the Kura were for the purpose of "forming insurmountable barriers, which obstructed the path of the migrating fish and forced them to assemble in huge crowds; the possibility of being caught by the rows of hooks placed before the *zabojka* was thus enhanced, so that the weir was rather of an auxiliary character than a fishing tool in the strict sense."[82]

The second volume of Šul'c's work contains a description of the manner in which fishermen of Astrakhan make their catch in the *učug* waters (учужные воды), that is in those portions of the river which are dammed up by weirs. He distinguishes three significant periods. The first lasts from early spring to the middle of July, thus covering the spawning time of Acipenseridae. Sturgeon at this time is caught exclusively by means of samolovs. The second is the autumn period, when fishing is done with the aid of nets; mainly sheatfish and carp are caught at this time, but occasionally sturgeon is captured also. Fishing during the third period, in winter when the fish are roused by alarm, is called *gromka* (громка).

It seems worthwhile to expatiate upon this last-named manner of fishing. The *gromka* has attained especial significance in the Kanič (a deep branch of

80. Данилевский (1871), p. 305.
81. Gmelin (1774–84), II, Pl. 36.
82. Шульц (1863), p. 45.
83. Шульц (1861), p. 57.

the Volga that joins another branch, the Kamizjak, in the delta), and also in the *učug* waters that used to be leased by contractors from the imperial treasury. Beginning at the sea, at the so-called Šarapov promontory, *gromka* operations extend along the whole length of the branch and come to a stop eight versts (8,5 km.) before the *učug*. The reason the *gromka* cannot be continued right up to the weir itself is that the area there is covered with innumerable hooks through all seasons. The whole stretch dedicated to the *gromka* is thus about 20 versts (21 km.) long. Making noise after the water has frozen is strictly prohibited along this stretch, and swimming is even prohibited earlier so as not to rouse the hibernating animals.

The usual time for the *gromka* is the middle of December, but that of 1853, for instance—the year Šul'c studied winter fishery in this region—was postponed by the contractor to January on account of inauspicious weather. The postponement was announced to all fishermen concerned, whether or not they were bound to the lessee by contract.

The *gromka* observed by Šul'c was attended by 350 fishermen, who had brought their sleds to the scene of operations. It was arranged by the inspector of the učug waters, and he convened the participants, both those who had their own tools and those who, as employees of the state, were to be provided with the necessary paraphernalia by their local inspectors. After fixing the point from which the *gromka* was to start, the central inspector determined the sequence of the participants by drawing lots. Having offered a prayer, the noisy crowd set out, each man carrying his sled loaded with tools. Arriving at the assigned spot, the inspector called the name of the lucky person who had won first place and showed him the point where he was to place his samolov or ахан (a huso net with meshes of 18-22 cm.) across the river. The man so summoned, got busy with his assistant without delay, while the others went farther along. The next fisherman's place was at a distance of 9 sažen (20 m.) from the first, and so on, until everybody got his place. This allocation of the fishermen is called *šapka* (шапка), and not more than two are set up on the same day.

As soon as the alignment of the participants was finished, a feverish activity set in all over the ice. While some persons were cleaning the surface with shovels or measuring the necessary distance by paces, others were chipping at the ice sheet and widening the holes for the fishing tools. Again, at some other point they were submerging the hooks or the net through the hole or pulling them from one hole to the other by means of guiding poles.

In a few hours, after having taken their chances in the first area, the fishermen reassembled around the leader and, when his signal was given, proceeded with great noise farther upstream to form the second *šapka*. This was arranged like the first and, as mentioned, no more than two were formed in the course of a day. The *gromka* was so continued for four or five days, until the entire apportioned stretch was exhausted.

This first *gromka* was followed by the "general" *gromka* (генеральная громка), in which the fishermen, instead of being huddled together, chose their places at discretion. Everybody set up his tools and caught fish where he wished without being commanded by the leader. The general *gromka* lasted two or three days, during which the whole stretch was covered in the opposite direction, that is, downstream.

Where the first *gromka* (upstream) and the "general" *gromka* (downstream) were in progress, smaller fish and such sturgeon as had succeeded in evading the tools of the fishermen and tried to escape to the sea were hunted down at the mouth of the river by means of six to ten dragnets (невода).

To get a true picture of the *gromka* one must add the ceaseless coming and going of a multitude of shouting children and the milling crowd of bustling women, some busy carrying the captured fish, others bringing food to their fathers or husbands, still others building a fire to cook fish soup, for which the most savory pieces of fish were used. The area of the gromka was surrounded by a host of buyers, who, together with their carriers, sometimes come from quite distant regions.

The *gromka* used to yield considerable profit, which benefited the lease holders most, since the fishermen themselves received comparatively low prices.[84]

Kuznecov gives but a general description of river fishery in Russia and repeats Šul'c's statement that "fish, accumulating before the weirs, are caught with hooks." It is only in passing that he mentions nets and weels placed in the openings of (presumably smaller) weirs.[85]

The same manner of fishery was demonstrated in the description of the Danubian anchor-shaped huso hooks given earlier. J. Alt's two lithographs (Figs. 16 and 17) show weirs on the lower Danube from the nineteenth century before which several rows of hooks are placed. These weirs had no device for catching fish other than the labyrinth of hooks floating in front of them.

There is a Hungarian analogy, although it had nothing to do with Acipenseridae. A structure, called *maráza* (Fig. 79) used to be employed along the upper stretches of the Tisza River at Beszterec; it was in many respects similar to the above-mentioned weirs with hooks in front. This contraption was employed for fishing in small lakes and ponds situated near the villages. The weir of the *maráza* consisted of a 15-meter-long *lésza*, that is, a wall of reed composed of three layers and held together by means of knitted hazel nut fibers or strings. The height of the *lésza* varied according to the depth of the water. The reeds forming the wall were so chosen that 64 centimeter (2 sukk) of their length could be driven into the bottom and still leave 75 centimeter (about half a fathom) emerging from the water.

After erecting the *lésza* at a suitable point, stakes were driven into the bottom around it. The distance between two neighboring stakes was 2 fathoms (3 m.), and that between the stakes and the *lésza* 1 sukk (32 cm.). A thin rope ("sinew") was stretched between the emerging portions of the stakes 1 sukk

84. *Ibid.*, pp. 58–60.
85. Kusnetzow (1898), p. 39.

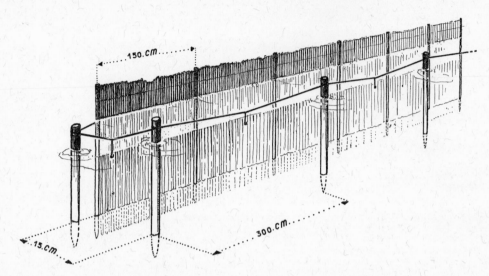

FIGURE 79.—Serially arranged hooks set up in front of a wall of reed *(maráza)* for the capture of small fish. The structure is, in principle, like that of hook rows placed before huso weirs. Beszterec, Rétköz (flood area of upper Tisza). (After Nyárády 's description.)

(32 cm.) above the surface of the water; strings ("auxiliary sinews") 2 sukks in length were suspended from the rope and hooks—made mostly of copper (!)—were tied to the ends of these auxiliary sinews. Small fish (mostly crucian carp), as in the case of the Russian *peremjot* were impaled on the hooks as bait. The point of the hook went through the back of the bait, which kept on writhing until a passing pike swallowed it.[86]

Worthy of mention is the fact that, like the Russian weirs, the *maráza* of Beszterec also had another variety in which the catching device was built into the reed wall by placing a fish basket of wickerwork between the layers. There were no stakes around the *lésza* and the hook line was fastened to the top of the fish basket, so the hooks came to lie round the weir in this case too.[87]

86. Nyárády (1938), pp. 162, 165, 167, and 171.
87. *Ibid.*, p. 167.

CHAPTER VIII

CONCLUSIONS AND OBSERVATIONS

This study of hooks of the samolov type has resulted in certain conclusions of a fundamental character, which go beyond the narrow frame of this monograph and concern ethnology in general and Eurasian historic piscatological research in particular. Apart from conclusions regarding general research, inferences about hooks of the samolov type only are possible. The following synopsis does not present a general summary rather its object is to lend emphasis to those fundamental findings which may have passed unnoticed among the foregoing details.

Samolov, a Bearer of Tradition

Mankind was born with a certain number of tools. Owing their existence to the very first ideas formed to satisfy man's primary needs, these tools were, by their very nature, so simple and perfect that they seemed to be incapable of further development ... A hook is a tool of this kind: its material may have been improved but its form is still the traditional one.

In these words Blanchère summed up his research into the history of hooks.

Simple as fishhooks are, they nevertheless reveal ancient morphological features that cannot be said to have been invented for promoting the efficacy of fishing. Let us remember that the different ways in which the shank and crook of hooks are bent often have nothing to do with the efficacy of the tool but rather are the expressions of tradition and usage characteristic of a circumscribed geographical unit. Not even the manufacturing industry is able to disregard local tradition, since its products must be so formed as to satisfy the taste of its customers, who insist on the maintenance of traditional forms.

Investigations of sturgeon hooks have well proved the extraordinary force of tradition. The comparative scrutiny of recent hooks of the samolov type reveals morphological features that are undoubtedly of prehistoric origin. For example, Type III of the Danubian huso hooks betrays traditional traces of neolithic bone hooks.

Traditional morphological features seem to be more pronounced in hooks of the samolov type than in other European fishhooks. This may be because samolovs have always been isolated from the morphological influence of other types. Their separate position is due to the fact, among others, that the use of sturgeon hooks has always been restricted to those rivers or those portions of rivers through which certain species of Acipenseridae passed in the course of their seasonal migrations. The employment of sturgeon hooks could, of course, never spread beyond the boundary of such seasonal runs, with the result that tools of this kind were never exposed to such alien influences as can, for instance, be observed in the interaction between pike hooks and sheatfishhooks.

A shape most suitable for the purpose they serve is naturally a decisive factor in the survival of hooks. Special biological properties of the sturgeon determined the development of a particular form and structure and also a special manner of manipulation of sturgeon hooks. The technique of sturgeon fishing is fundamentally different from other fishing methods, and it is due to this difference that the boundary between samolovs and other hooks was always sharp, even within the limits of a restricted area, a factor undoubtedly conducive to the survival of tradition.

The principle underlying fishing with samolovs reveals traces of an ancient tradition that is of fundamental significance for theories regarding the general evolution of fishhooks. The following considerations have led to this conclusion.

Wooden hooks, with their natural buoyancy, must be regarded as the most ancient type of the samolov. Logical reasoning and a morphological comparison with prehistoric bone hooks lead to the supposition that all kinds of hooks may be traced back to wooden hooks. The material of this archetype insured the natural buoyancy of the prehistoric hooks, and only subsequent experience made it clear that it was more expedient to sink, below the surface those hooks which were intended to catch fish other than sturgeon. The samolov is the only floating hook among recent European metal hooks, so hooks of the samolov type seem to be the only survivals of the prehistoric model.

The Origin of Samolovs

J. Jankó champions the theory that hooks of the samolov type are of southeastern European Turko-Tataric origin. Lappic samolovs of the Viking period seem to disprove this hypothesis; therefore a more likely theory is that hooks of the samolov type originated in northern Europe or, at least, the northern part of Eurasia. This theory relies chiefly on the principle that governs the technique of catching fish, while morphological considerations also seem to support it.

Since there are apparently no similar indications for eastern Asiatic samolovs it is not possible to advance a reliable theory of their genesis.

Diffusion of Samolovs on the Lower (Balkan) Danube

The bronze huso hook from the early Iron Age found at Ispánlaka and the description of Aelianus make it clear that single (i.e., not serially suspended) huso hooks were already used in antiquity. Samolovs as used nowadays— rows of serially suspended large hooks—were introduced by Ukrainian and Russian refugees, the ancestors of the present Lipovans, who arrived at the Danube in several waves between 1655 and 1856. Sterlet hooks of the samolov type became popular in the course of the last century.

Diffusion of Samolovs on the Middle (Hungarian) Danube

The middle portion of the Danube River extends from the Iron Gate to Pozsony, and it was sometime after 1840 that rows of samolov hooks came into use there. The path for the spread of samolovs was probably opened by the regulation of the Iron Gate, when their natural transmitters, boatmen and fishermen, were abled to navigate upstream without hindrance. Jankó's theory that hooks of the samolov type were imported to the middle Danube by the conquering Magyars who occupied the Carpathian Basin in the ninth century is evidently untenable.

Chronology of Implements Used for Fishing for Acipenseridae

The history and chronological sequence of the different tools used in sturgeon fishery is strikingly similar along the rivers of the southern Russian plain and the Danube. In a chronological table, tools used for great sturgeon fishing must be treated separately from those employed in sterlet fishery. The following table is an attempt at presenting their evolutionary sequence.

Huso and Other Large Sturgeon		Sterlet
Hafted crook or harpoon	before	Wicker weel
Single-layered dragnet	weirs or	Three-layered swimming net
Floated samolov	independently	Samolov
Floatless samolov		
Floatless baited hanging samolov		

Since the present work is a study of hooks, proofs in substantiation of this scheme should not be adduced. The foregoing outline is all that is needed to establish the role played by fishhooks in the ethnology of sturgeon fishery.

Speculative reasoning leads to the assumption that the active form of sturgeon fishing with single hooks tied to thin ropes was derived from sturgeon fishing with hafted crooks. It must be remembered that sturgeon is sometimes caught in the winter season with single hooks and simple crooks in much the same way. Holes are cut in the ice, and the hook is first let down through them and then jerked upward with the same movements that would be used if it were a simple crook. In other words, both hook and crook are weapons of attack in this case, and not mere passive tools that leave it to the fish to impale itself.

Such considerations would have justified the ethnological study of hafted sturgeon crooks within the frame of this monograph. The history of hafted crooks constitutes, however, a quite separate complex, and its analysis must be left to another time.

Primacy of Rivers against the Sea in Sturgeon Fishery

That this monograph is almost exclusively concerned with sturgeon hooks used in river fishery is due to certain historical factors.

Sturgeon fishery in the sea is nowadays by no means inferior in size and significance to that in the river. It should, however, be remembered that during historical times systematic sturgeon fishery was always confined to rivers and estuaries rich in this kind of fish. Sturgeon fishery on a large scale in the Black Sea and the Caspian Sea began only at the end of the eighteenth century, together with the industrialization of fishing. That this is historically true is evidenced by the fact that certain traditional archaic features of sturgeon fishery can best be observed on the rivers. Only up-to-date tools and fishing methods are encountered on the seashores, and they are of only secondary interest for the student of ethnology.

Historico-ethnological researches are constantly accumulating data to prove that fishery in Eurasia began on the inland waters of the continent, spread from them first to the estuaries of the rivers and the bays and inlets of the sea, to conquer subsequently—as a matter of fact, in comparatively recent times—the vast expanse of the seas.

BIBLIOGRAPHY

AELIANUS, CLAUDIUS

1864–66. "Περὶ ζῴων ἰδιότητος" In: *Claudii Aeliani de natura animalium libri XVII* ... Ex recognitione RUDOLPHI HERSCHERI. 2 vols. Bibliotheca scriptorum graecorum et romanorum teubneriana. Lipsiae. (In Greek.)

AHLQUIST, AUG[UST]

1885. "Unter Wogulen und Ostjaken. Reisebriefe und ethnographische Mitteilungen." In: *Acta Societatis Scientiarum Fennicae*, XIV, 133–307. Helsingfors.

Amtliche Bericht über die Internationale Fischerei-Ausstellung zu Berlin 1880. 1881. Vol. II. Berlin.

АНДРЕЕВ, Ал.

1922. "Риболовство в Никополско" ("Fishing at Nikopoli"), Известия на Народният Этнографски Музей в София ("Review of the National Ethnographical Museum of Sofia"), II, 118–31. София.. (In Bulgarian.)

ANELL, BENGT

1955. *Contribution to the History of Fishing in the Southern Seas.* ("Studia ethnographica upsaliensia," Vol. 9.) Uppsala.

ANTIPA, GR.

1916. *Pescăria şi pescuitul in România* ("Fishing and Fishermen inRumania"). Bucureşti. (In Rumanian.)

ARNAUD, ODETTE

1935. "Les Lipovans du Danube, pêcheurs de caviars," *Bulletin de la Société des Amis du Muséum d'Histoire Naturelle*, n.s., No. 13, pp. 23-25. Paris.
1936. *Pêcheurs de rêves*, ("La vie d'aujourd'hui," Vol. 42.) Paris.

ASZTRAKÁN

1858. *Vasárnapi Ujság*, V, 234. Budapest. (In Hungarian.)

BAER, CARL ERNST VON

1853. "Materialien zu einer Geschichte des Fischfanges in Russland und den angrenzenden Meeren." In: *Mélanges biologiques tirés du Bulletin de l'Académie Impériale des Sciences de Saint-Pétersbourg*, XI, 568–632. Saint-Pétersbourg.
v. i.: БЭР, К. М. фон.

BEASLEY, HARRY G.

1928. *Pacific Island Records: Fish Hooks.* Seeley.

BELÉNYESY, MÁRTA

1953. "A halászat a XIV. században" ("Fishing in the fourteenth Century"), *Ethnographia*, LXIV, 148–64. Budapest. (In Hungarian.)

БЭР, К. М. Фон

1860. Рыболовство въ Каспийскомъ море и въ его притокахъ ("Fishing on the Caspian Sea and Its Tributaries"). ("Изследования о состоянии рыболовства въ России" ["Research on the State of Fishing in Russia"], Vol. II.) Санктпетербургъ. (In Russian.)

BERG, L. S.

1932. "Übersicht der Verbreitung der Süsswasserfische Europas," *Zoogeographica*, I, 107–208. Jena.
v. i.: Промысловые

BLANCHÈRE, HENRI DE LA

1885. *La pêche et les poissons*. Paris.

BONNERJEA, BIREN

1939. "Fish-Hooks in North America and Their Distribution, Based Principally on Museum Collections," *Journal of the Indian Anthropological Institute*, I, 69–147. Calcutta.
1939–40. "La pêche chez les peuples finno-ougriens," *L'Anthropologie*, XLIX, 661–96. Paris.

BORODIN, N[IKOLAJ ANDREEVIČ]

1893. *The Ural Cossacks and Their Fisheries*. New York.

BORODINE, N. A. [BORODIN, NIKOLAJ ANDREEVIČ]

1913. "Pêche et pisciculture en Russie." In: *Atti del V. Congresso Internationale di Pesca*, 1911. Roma.

BOUILLET, MARIE NICOLAS

1893. *Dictionnaire universel d'histoire et de géographie*. Paris.

BRØGGER, A. W.

1907. "Vistefundet: En aeldre stenalders kjøkkenmødding fra Jaederen" ("The Find at Viste: A Kitchen-Midden of Jaederen from the Early Stone Age"). *Stavangers Museums Aarshefte*, XVIII, Part II, 1–102. Stavanger. (In Norwegian.)
1910. "Fortegnelse over de til Stavanger Museum i 1910 indkomne saker aeldre end Reformationen" ("Specification of the Objects from before the Reformation Acquired in the Stavanger Museum"). *Stavangers Museums Aarshefte*, XXI, Part V, 1–45. Stavanger. (In Norwegian.)

Брусов, А. Я.

1952. Очерки по истории племен Европейской части СССР в неолитическую эпоху ("Studies on the History of the European Part of the USSR during the Neolithic Age"). Москва. (In Russian.)

BUCH, LEOPOLD VON

1870. *Reise durch Norwegen und Lappland*. 2 vols. Berlin, 1810. *Gesammelte Schriften*, II, 109–563. Berlin.

CHRISTENSEN

1881. "Zur Geschichte des Angelhakens," *Deutsche Fischereizeitung*, IV, Stettin.

CLARK, J. G[RAHAM] D.

1948. "The Development of Fishing in Prehistoric Europe," *Antiquaries Journal*, XXVIII, 45–85. Oxford.
1952. *Prehistoric Europe: The Economic Basis*. London.

ĆURČIĆ, VEJSIL

1910–15. "Narodno ribarstvo u Bosni i Hercegovini" ("Popular Fishing in Bosnia and Herzegovina"), *Glasnik Zemaljskog Muzeja u Bosni i Hercegovini* ("Bulletin of the Regional Museum of Bosnia and Herzegovina"), XXII (1910), 379–487; XXV (1913), 421–513; XXVII (1915), 37–107, 313–58. Sarajevo. (In Croatian.)

DABRY DE THIERSANT, [CLAUDE PHILIBERT]

1872. *La pisciculture et la pêche en Chine.* Paris.

DANILEWSKY, C. [DANILEVSKIJ, N. JA.]

1867. *Coup d'œil sur les pêcheries en Russie.* Paris.

Данилевский, Н. Я.

1860. Описание Уралскаго рыболовства ("Description of Uralian Fishing"). ("Изследования о состоянии рыболовства въ России" ["Research on the State of Fishing in Russia"], Vol. III.) Санктпетербургъ. (In Russian.)
1862. Рыбные и зверные промыслы на Беломъ и Ледовитомъ моряхъ ("Piscicultural and Animal Exploitation on the White and Frozen Seas"). *Ibid.*, Vol. VI.
1863. Статистика Каспийскаго рыболовства ("Statistics on Caspian Fishing"). *Ibid.*, Vol. V.

1871. Описание рыболовства на Черномъ и Азовскомъ моряхъ ("Description of Fishing on the Black and Azov Seas"). *Ibid.*, Vol. VIII. Figure-album to this volume: Рисунки къ изследованию рыболовства на Черномъ и Азовскомъ моряхъ ("Drawings Illustrating the Research of Fishing on the Black and Azov Seas").
1875. Описание рыболовства въ Северо-Западныхъ Озерахъ ("Descripstion of Fishing on the North-West Lakes"). *Ibid.*, Vol. IX.

DIETRICH, KARL

1912. *Byzantinische Quellen zur Länder- und Völkerkunde (5–15 Jhd).* Leipzig.

Donau Ansichten nach dem Laufe des Donaustromes ....

1826. Lithographs by JAKOB ALT, text by GEORG CARL BORROMÄUS RUMY, ed. ADOLF KUNIKE. Wien.

DUMITRESCU, HORTENSIA

1935–36. Objets inédits du dépôt en bronze de Spalnaca, au Musée National des Antiquités de Bucarest," *Dacia*, V–VI, 195–224. Bucureşti.

DÜBEN, GUSTAV

1873. *Om Lappland och Lapparne, företrädesvis de Svenske* ("About Lapland and the Laps, Mainly Swedish"). Stockholm. (In Swedish.)

EBERT, MAX

1921. *Südrussland im Altertum.* Bonn.
1924–32. *Reallexikon der Vorgeschichte.* Vols. I–XV. Berlin.

ECSEDI, ISTVÁN

1933. "Népies halászat a Közép-Tiszán és a tiszántúli kisvizeken" ("Popular Fishing on the Middle Tisza and in the Small Waters beyond the Tisza").

In: *Déri Múzeum Évkönyve* ("Year Book of the Déri Museum"), pp. 123–308. Debrecen. (In Hungarian.)

EMORY, KENNETH P., WILLIAM J. BONK, and YOSIHOKO H. SINOTO
1959. *Fishhooks*, ("Hawaiian Archaeology. Bernice P. Bishop Museum Special Publication," Vol. XLVII.) Honolulu.

Эварницкий, Д. И.
1892. История запорожскихъ Козаков ("History of the Zaporozhian Cossacks"), Vol. I. Санктпетербуръ. (In Russian.)

FALTAY, LÁSZLÓ
1915. "Vizahorgászat a Duna-deltában" ("Angling for Huso in the Danube Delta"). *Halászat* ("Fishing"), XVI, 106–9. Budapest. (In Hungarian.)

GAÁL, KÁROLY
1947. "A gutai 'rekeszt' és a vizafogó cége" ("The 'Rekeszt' of Guta and the Huso-Weir"), *Ethnographia*, LVIII, 252–57. Budapest. (In Hungarian.)

GHELASE, GH. I.
1951. *Uneltele de pescuit și confecționarea lor* ("Fishing Tools and Their Making"). București. (In Rumanian.)

GJESSING, GUTORM
1945. *Norges Stenalder* ("The Norwegian Stone Age"). Oslo. (In Norwegian.)

GLOB, P. V.
1952. *Yngre Stenalder* ("The Late Stone Age"). ("Danske oldsager" ["Danish Antiquities"], Vol. II.) København. (In Danish.)

GMELIN, SAMUEL GOTTLIEB
1774–84. *Reise durch Russland zur Untersuchung der drey Naturreiche . . . .* 4 tomes in 3 vols. St. Petersburg.

GROSSINGER, JOANNES BAPT.
1794. *Universa historia physica Regni Hungariae secundum tria regna naturae digesta*, Vol. III. *Regni animalis*, Part III. *Ichthyologia, sive historia piscium et amphibiorum*. Posonii et Comaromii.

GRUVEL, A.
1928. *La pêche dans la préhistoire, dans l'antiquité et chez les peuples primitifs*. Paris.

Гурина, Н. Н.
1953. "Памятники эпохи раннего металла на' северном побережье Кольского полуострова" ("Monuments from the Early Metallic Age on the Northern Coast of the Peninsula of Kola"). In: А. П. Окладников, Палеолит и неолит СССР ("USSR Paleolithic and Neolithic"), pp. 347-407. Москва. (In Russian.)

HADDON, A. C., and JAMES HORNELL
1936–38 *Canoes of Oceania*. 3 vols. ("Bernice P. Bishop Museum Special Publication." Vols. XXVII–XXIX.) Honolulu.

HAMPEL, JÓZSEF
1896. *A bronzkor emlékei Magyarhonban* ("Relics of the Bronze Age in Hungary"). 3 vols. Budapest. (In Hungarian.)

HASSLÖFF, OLOF
1949. *Svenska västkustfiskarna* ("The Swedish Fishermen of the West Coast"). Göteborg. (In Swedish.)

HECKEL, J. J.
1863. "Magyarország édesvizi halainak rendszeres átnézete, jegyzetekkel s az uj fajok rövid leírásával" ("A Systematic Survey of Hungary's Fresh-Water Fishes, with Notes and a Short Description of New Species"). Fordította s bővítette ("Translated and Amplified by") KORNÉL CHYZER. In: GEJZA HALÁSZ, *A magyar orvosok és természetvizsgálók 1847 ... Sopronban tartott VIII. nagygyűlésének történeti vázlata és és munkálatai* ("Historical Outline and Agenda of the 8th Congress of Hungarian Physicians and Naturalists Held at Sopron, 1847"), pp. 193–216. Pest. (In Hungarian.)

HERMAN, OTTÓ
1885. *Ösi nyomok a magyar népies halászatban* ("Archaic Features in Hungarian Fishery"). Budapest. (In Hungarian.)
1887. *A magyar halászat könyve* ("Book of Hungarian Fishery"). 2 vols. Budapest. (In Hungarian.)
1893. *Az északi madárhegyek tájáról* ("From the Land of the Northern Bird Hills"). Budapest. (In Hungarian.)
1900. *Die Forschungsreisen der Grafen Eugen Zichy in Asien: Dritte Reise.* Band I. Budapest.
—— Notebooks in manuscript, Vol. IV. In the Archives of the Ethnographical Museum of Budapest, No. EA 000182/4. (In Hungarian.)

HERODOTOS
1909. *Herodoti historiarum libri IX.* Ed. HENR. RUDOLPH. DIETSCH. Editio altera, Vol. I. Bibliotheca scriptorum graecorum et romanorum teubneriana. Lipsiae. (In Greek.)

HOSMER, DOROTHY
1940. "Caviar Fishermen of Romania: From Vâlcov, 'Little Venice' of the Danube Delta, Bearded Russian Exiles Go Down to the Sea," *National Geographic Magazine*, LXXVII, 407–34. Washington.

INDREKO, R.
1937. *Über die vorgeschichtliche Fischerei in Estland.* ("Abhandlungen der Fischereikammer," Vol. II.) Tallinn.
1948. *Die mittlere Steinzeit in Estland.* ("Kungl. Vitterhets Historie och Antikvites Akademiens Handlingar," Vol. LXVI.) Uppsala.

JANKÓ, JÁNOS
1900. *A magyar halászat eredete—Herkunft der magyarischen Fischerei.* 2 vols. ("Zichy Jenő gróf harmadik ázsiai utazása—Dritte asiatische Forschungsreise des Grafen Eugen Zichy," Tome 1.) Budapest. (Hungarian—German bilingual ed.)

—— Notebooks in manuscript. In the Archives of the Ethnographical Museum of Budapest. (In Hungarian.)

Калебъ, О.

1863. Каспийскомъ рыболовстве ["Fishing on the Caspian Sea"]. Санктпетербургъ. (In Russian.)

KELLER, FERDINAND

1865–66. *Die keltischen Phalbauten in den schweizer Seen.* Zürich.

KHIN, ANTAL

1928. "A csallóközi vizahalászat" ("Huso Fishing in the Csallóköz"). In: *Csallóközi Múzeum,* ed. ZOLTÁN JANKÓ, pp. 50–54. Bratislava. (In Hungarian.)
1936. "A csallóközi vizák" ("The Huso of the Csallóköz"), *Szülőföldünk,* I, 41–43. Bratislava—Pozsony. (In Hungarian.)

K. MÁTYUS, ISTVÁN

1787. *Ó és Uj Diaetetica az az: Az . . . Istentől adatott nevezetesebb Természeti Eszközöknek . . . elé-számlálása* ("Old and New Dietetics, or: Account of Notable Natural Tools Given by God"). Vol. III. Posony. (In Hungarian.)

KOEHLER, HEINRICH [HEINRICH KARL ERNST KÖHLER]

1832. "Τάριχος ou recherches sur l'histoire et sur les antiquités des pêcheries de la Russie méridionale." In *Mémoires de l'Académie Impériale des Sciences de Saint-Pétersbourg.* 6th ser. I, 347–490. Saint-Pétersbourg.

Колчин, Б. А.

1953/A. Черная металлургия и металлообработка в древней Руси: Домонголской период "(Black Metallurgy and Metallic Works in Old Russia: Premongolian Period"). ("Материалы и Исследования по Археологии СССР" ["Materials and Studies on the Archaeology of the USSR"] Vol. XXXII.) Москва. (In Russian.)
1953/B Техника обработки металла в древней Руси ["Metallic Work Technology in Old Russia"]. Москва. [In Russian.]

KOMORÓCZY, GYÖRGY

1932. *Nádasdi Tamás és a XVI. századi magyar nagybirtok gazdálkodása* ("Tamás Nádasdi, and Husbandry on the Hungarian Latifundia in the sixteenth Century"). ("Tanulmányok a magyar mezőgazdaság történetéhez" [Studies on the History of Hungarian Agriculture"], Vol. III.) Budapest. (In Hungarian.)

KOUDRIAVTSEV, P.

1893. "Les vestiges de l'homme préhistorique de l'âge de la pierre près du village Volosova, district et gouvernement de Vladimir." In: *Congrès International d'Archéologie et d'Anthropologie Préhistorique, 11ème session à Moscou, 1892,* II, 233–62. Moscou.

KRAUSE, EDUARD

1897. "Vorgeschichtliche Fischereigeräte und neuere Vergleichsstücke", *Globus,* LXXI, 265–75 and 289–92. Braunschweig.
1904. "Vorgeschichtliche Fischereigeräte und neuere Vergleichsstücke, *Zeitschrift für Fischerei,* IX, 133–300. Berlin.

KRISCH, ANTON
1900. "Die Fischerei im Adriatischen Meere mit besonderer Berücksichtigung der österreichisch-ungarischen Küsten." Sonderabdruck aus *Mitteilungen aus dem Gebiete des Seewesens*. Pola.

KUSNETZOW, I. D.
1898. *Fischerei und Thiererbeutung in den Gewässern Russlands*. St. Petersburg.

LEIST, A.
1865. Von Baja bis Mehadia, *Globus*, VII, 193–201. Hildburghausen.

LEPECHIN, IWAN
1774–75. *Tagebuch der Reise durch verschiedene Provinzen des Russischen Reiches in den Jahren 1768 und 1769*. 2 vols. Altenburg.

LEROI–GOURHAN, ANDRÉ
1943. *L'homme et la matière: Évolution et techniques I*. ("Sciences d'aujourd'hui.") Paris.

LIBAY, JOSEPHUS
1788. *Copailicher neu accurat und noch niemalen in offentlicher Expression heraus gegebener pacticirter Donau Strohm*. ... Map in the cartographic collection of the Szechenyi Library of Budapest, inv. No.: T af 3.

LUKÁCS, KÁROLY
1953. "Adatok a Fertö és a Rábaköz halászatának történetéhez," *Ethnographia*, LXIV, 282–90. Budapest. (In Hungarian.)

MAGNIN ÉTIENNE
1959. "Répartition actuelle des Acipenseridés", *Revue des travaux de l'Institut des Pêches Maritimes*, XXIII, 277–85. Paris.

MANNINEN, ILMARI
1932. *Die finnisch-ugrischen Völker*. Leipzig.
1934. Kalastus ("Fishery"). In: *Suomen suku* ("The Finnish Kinship"), III, 47–72. Helsingissä. (In Finnish.)

Маргаритов, В. П.
1888. Объ Орочахъ императорской гавани ("About Imperial Orochon Harbors"). Санктпетербургъ. (In Russian.)

MARQUART, J[OSEF]
1903. *Osteuropäische und ostasiatische Streifzüge. Ethnologische und historisch-topographische Studien zur Geschichte des 9. und 10. Jahrhunderts*. Leipzig.

MATHIASSEN, THERKEL
1930. *Archaeological Collections from the Western Eskimos: Report of the Fifth Thule Expedition 1921–1924*, Vol. X, No. 1. Copenhagen.

MÁTYUS *see* K. MÁTYUS

MORI, TAMEZO
1936. *Studies on the Geographical Distribution of Freshwater Fishes in Eastern Asia.* Keijo.

MORR, JOSEF
1926. *Die Quellen von Strabons drittem Buch. Philologus,* Tome 18, Vol. III, suppl. Leipzig.

MORVAY, PÉTER
1948. Milyen volt az egykori vizafogó? ("What Was the Former Huso-Weir Like?"), *Ethnographia,* LIX, 88–94. Budapest. (In Hungarian.)

MOYNET, M.
1867. "Le Volga." In: *Le tour du monde,* XV, 49–96. Paris.

MUNKÁCSI, BERNÁT
1893. "A magyar népies halászat műnyelve" ("Technical Language of Hungarian Fishery"), *Ethnographia,* IV, 165–208, 261–313. Budapest. (In Hungarian.)

MUNRO, NEIL GORDON
1911. *Prehistoric Japan.* Yokohama.

MUNRO, ROBERT
1890. *The Lake-Dwellings of Europe.* London.

NICOLAYSEN, N.
1866. *Norske Fornlevninger* ("Norwegian Antiquities"). Kristiania. (In Norwegian.)

NOUGIER, LOUIS-RENÉ, and ROMAIN ROBERT
1951. "Hameçons néolithiques," *Bulletin de la Société Préhistorique Française,* XLVIII, 307–22.

N. SZABÓ, GYULA
1926. *Zalaország* ("The Zala Land"). Zalaegerszeg. (In Hungarian.)

NYÁRÁDY, MIHÁLY
1938. "A Rétköz régi halászata" ("Old-Time Fishery in the Rétköz)", *Ethnographia,* LXIX 156–74, 380–94. Budapest. (In Hungarian.)

NYIRI, ANTAL
1946–47. "A kihaló szentesi viziélet néprajzi és népnyelvi maradványai" ("Ethnographical and Linguistic Relics of the Declining Aquatic Life at Szentes"). In: *Alföldi Tudományos Gyüjtemény* [Scientific Miscellaneous of the Alföld"], II, 194–301. Szeged. (In Hungarian.)

Окладников, А. П.
1950. Неолит и бронзовый век Прибайкалья ("Neolithic and Bronze Ages in the Lake Baikal Region"). ("Материалы и Исследования по Археологии СССР" ["Materials and Studies on the Archeology of the USSR"], Vol. XVIII.) Москва. (In Russian).

OLAH, NICOLAUS

1735. "Hungaria." In: MATHIAS BÉL, *Adparatus ad Historiam Hungariae.* Posonii. (In Latin.)

PALLAS, P[ETER] S[IMON]

1771–76. *Reise durch verschiedene Provinzen des Russischen Reiches*, 3 vols. St. Petersburg.

PAULY, AUGUST FRIEDRICH, GEORG WISSOWA, WILHELM KROLL, and KARL MITTELHAUS

1894–1959. *Real-Encyclopädie der klassischen Altertumswissenschaft.* 56 vols. Stuttgart.

PÄLSI, SAKARI

1912. "Über steinzeitliche Hakenfischereigeräte in Finland," *Suomen Muinaismuistoyhdistyksen Aikakauskirja*, ("Review of the Finnish Archaeological Society"), XXVI, 195–204. Helsinki.

PELLEGRIN, JACQUES

1925. "Les esturgeons du Danube", *Bulletin de la Société Centrale d'Aquiculture et de Pêche*, XXXII, 97–107. Paris.

Петровић, Михаил

1941. Ђердапски риболови у прошлости и салашњьости ("Past and Present Fishing at the Iron-Gates"). "Српска Кральевска Академија, Српски Етнографски Эборник" ["Serbian Royal Academy, Serbian Ethnographical Review"], Tome 57, sec. 2, Vol. XXIV.) Београд. (In Serbian.)

PITTARD, EUGÈNE

1902. *Dans la Dobrodja.* Genève.

Промысловые рыбы СССР ("USSR Industrial Fish").

1949. Ed. Л. С. Берг, А. С. Богданов, Н. И. Кожин and Г. Расс. Москва. (In Russian.)

RAU, CHARLES

1884. *Prehistoric Fishing in Europe and North America.* Washington.

REINER, ZSIGMOND

1888. "Az ispánlaki bronzlelet" ("The Bronze Find of Ispánlaka"), *Archaeológiai Értesítö*, VIII, 10–25. Budapest. (In Hungarian.)

ROHAN–CSERMAK, GÉZA DE

1955. "A néprajztudós Herman Ottó" ("Ottó Herman as Ethnographer"), *Ethnographia*, LXVI, 487-500. Budapest. (In Hungarian, with large German summary.)
1956. *A magyar hajózás multjából* ("From the Past of the Hungarian Navigation"). Budapest. (In Hungarian, with large French summary.)
1959. 'Aspects historiques de la technique des instruments de métal pour la pêche en Europe centrale," *Folk-Liv—Acta ethnologica et folkloristica Europaea*, XXIII, 5–13. Stockholm.

RÓMER, FLÓRIS

——Notebooks in manuscript. (In Hungarian.)

Росс, М. Е.

—— Каргополская культура ("The Kargopol Culture"). Dissertation in the Archives of the University of Moscow. (In Russian.)

Rostami, Ismail

1961. *Biologie et exploitation des esturgeons (Acipenseridés) caspiens.* Bar-le-Duc (Meuse, France).

Сабанеев, Л. И.

1892. Рыбы России ["Fish of Russia"]. 2 vols. Москва. (In Russian.)

Sakazov, Ivan

1929. *Bulgarische Wirtschaftsgeschichte.* Berlin.

Scaliger, Julius Caesar

1557. *Exotericarum exercitationum liber quintus decimus, de subtilitate, ad Hieronymum Cardanum.* ... Lutetiae.

Schrenck, Leopold von

1881–1895. *Reisen und Forschungen im Amur-Lande.* Vol. III. *Die Völker des Amur Landes.* St. Petersburg.

Seligo, Artur

1926. "Die Fischerei in den Fliessen, Seen und Strandgewässern Mitteleuropas." In: R. Demoll and H. N. Maier, *Handbuch der Binnenfischerei Mitteleuropas,* V, 1–422. Stuttgart.

Shetelig, Haakon

1926. *Préhistoire de la Norvège.* Oslo.

Shetelig, Haakon, and Hjalmar Falk

1937. *Scandinavian Archaeology.* Oxford.

Silvestru, Radu

1936. "La Dobrugia," *L'Universo,* XVII, 103–28. Firenze. (In Italian.)

Sirelius, Uuno Taavi

1906. *Über die Sperrfischerei bei den finnisch-ugrischen Völkern.* Helsingfors. 1934. *Jagd und Fischerei in Finnland.* ("Die Volkskultur Finnlands," Vol. I.) Berlin.

Skinner, H. D.

1915. "Evolution of the Tautau, a Maori Pendant," *Man,* Vol. XV, article 2. London.

Solberg, O[le Martin]

1909. *Eisenzeitfunde aus Ostfinmarken. Lappländische Studien.* ("Skrifter udgivne af Videnskabs-Selskabet i Christiania," II. "Historisk Filosofisk Klasse." Vol. VII.) Christiania.

Stefan, Gh.

1937–40. "Dinogetia I," *Dacia,* VII–VIII, 401–25. Bucureşti. (In French.)

STRABON
1907. Γεωγραφικά. *Strabonis Geographica.* Recognovit AUGUST MEINEKE. 3 vols. Bibliotheca scriptorum graecorum et romanorum teubneriana. Lipsiae. (In Greek.)

STRAHLENBERG, PHILIPP JOHANN VON
1730. *Das Nord- und Ostliche Theil von Europa und Asia.* Stockholm.

Шульц, А. Я.
1861. Техническое описание Каспийскаго рыболовства ("Technical Description of the Caspian Fishing".) ("Изследования о состоянии рыболовства въ России" ["Research on the State of Fishing in Russia"], Vol. 4.) Figure-album to this volume: Рисунки къ изследованию Каспийскаго рыболовства ("Drawings Illustrating the Research on the Caspian Fishing"). Санктпетербургъ. (In Russian.)
1863. Техническое описание рыбныхъ и звериныхъ промысловъ на Беломъ и Ледовитомъ моряхъ ("Technical Description of Piscicultural and Animal Exploitation on the White and Frozen Seas"). *Ibid.*, Vol. 7. Figure-album to this volume: Рисунки къ изследованию рыбныхъ и звериныхъ промысловъ на Беломъ и Ледовитомъ моряхъ ("Drawings Illustrating the Research on the Piscicultural and Animal Exploitation on the White and Frozen Seas") Санктпетербургъ. (In Russian.)

SZABÓ, GYULA *See* N. SZABÓ, GYULA

SZABÓ, KÁLMÁN
1937. "A Kecskeméti Múzeum halászati gyüjteménye" ("The Popular Fishing Collection of the Museum at Kecskemét"), *Néprajzi Értesítő*, XXIX, 136–63, 376–415. Budapest. (In Hungarian.)

SZAMOTA, ISTVÁN
1894. "Természetrajzi és halászati nevek régi okiratokban 1600-ig. Halászat" ["Terms of Natural History and Fishery in Old Documents to 1600: Fishing"], *Természettudományi Közlöny*, XXVI, 491–95. Budapest. (In Hungarian.)

SZINNYEI, JÓZSEF
1863. "Adatok Rév-Komárom halászatához" ("Contribution to the Fishing of Rév-Komárom"). *Vasárnapi Ujság*, X, 119, 130–31. Budapest. (In Hungarian.)

SZURMAY, SÁNDOR
1926. "A kecsege és a tokfélék: Fogás és tenyésztés" ("The Sterlet and the Acipenseridae: Catching and Cultivation"). *Halászat* ("Fishery"), XXVII, 44–46. Budapest. (In Hungarian.)

TAKÁTS, SÁNDOR
1897. "A komáromi vizahalászat a XVI. században" ("Huso Fishing at Komárom in the sixteenth Century"). *Magyar Gazdaságtörténelmi Szemle* ("Review of Hungarian Economic History"), IV, 425–45 and 485–509. Budapest. (In Hungarian.)

Танасийчук, Н. П.
1951. Промысловые рыбы Болго-Каспия ("Volgo-Caspian Industrial Fish"). Москва. (In Russian.)

TAUBE, FRIEDRICH WILHELM

1777. *Beschreibung des Königreiches Slavonien und des Herzogthumes Syrmien.* Vol. I. Leipzig.

TÉGLÁS, GÁBOR

1887. "Az ispánlaki nagy bronzlelet" ("The Great Bronze Find of Ispánlaka") *Erdélyi Múzeum*, IV, 331–34. Kolozsvár. (In Hungarian.)

THOMAZI, A.

1947. *Histoire de la pêche des âges de la pierre à nos jours.* Bibliothèque historique. Paris.

Ушаков, Д. Н.

1939–41. Толковый словарь русского языка ("Analytical Dictionnary of the Russian Language"). 3 vols. Москва. (In Russian.)

Варпаховский, Н. А.

1898. Рыболовство въ бассейне, реки Оби. Vol. I. Орудия рыболовства и продукты рыбнаго промысла "(Fishing in the Basin of the Ob River," Vol. I. "Piscicultural Means of Production and Products"). Санктпетербургъ. (In Russian.)

VILKUNA, KUSTAA

1953–54. "Laxfisket som helhetsproblem i Norden" ("Salmon Fishing as a Whole Problem in the North"), *Svenska Landsmål och Svenskt Folkliv*, I–VIII, 245–52. Stockholm. (In Swedish.)
1956. "Lachsfang als Gesamtproblem", *Actes du IVème Congrès International des Sciences Anthropologiques et Ethnologiques, Vienne, 1952*, III, 87–90. Wien.

Воронин, Н. Н.

1954. Древнее Гродно ("The Former Grodno"). ("Материалы и Исследования по Археологии СССР" ["Materials and Studies on the Archeology of the USSR"], Vol. XLI.) Москва. (In Russian.)

Бовк, Хв.*

1899. "Українське рибальство у Добруджі" ("Ukrainian Fishery in Dobruja"). Материяли до Українсько-Руськo Этнольогії ("Materials on Ukraino-Russian Ethnology"), Vol. I. Львів. (In Ukrainian.)

VULPE, RADU, and ECATERINA VULPE

1924. Les fouilles de Tinosul, *Dacia*, I, 166-223. Bucureşti.

ZEGA, NIKOLA

1926–27. "Ribolov na Donjem Dunavu" ("Fishing on the Lower Danube"), *Etnolog*, I, 36–40. Ljubljana. (In Slovenian.)

ZNAMIEROWSKA-PRÜFFEROWA, MARIA

1957. *Rybackie narzędzia kolne w Polsce i w krajach sąsiednich* ("Thrusting Implements for Fishing in Poland and the Neighbouring Countries"). ("Studia Societatis Scientiarum Torunensis," Vol. "Supplement" IV.) Toruń. (In Polish, with large English summary.)

* This author writes his name "Volkov" in latin characters (cf. French summary and contents of the cited review).

Other sources include the data collected by the author along the Danube, at Komárom, Dunapentele, Tolna, and Mohács, and also along the Tisza, at Tokaj in particular.

Acknowledgment is due the excellent dictionaries of BAILLY and LIDDEL–SCOTT, which helped in the correct interpretation of Greek texts. Also to be mentioned are those monographs on fishhooks that—though not as sources furnishing us with data incorporated in the present work—rendered valuable assistance by their guidance in the matter of methodology. The very subjects of these monographs justify their following enumeration.

BLAKEY, ROBERT

1856. *Historical Sketches of the Angling Literature of all Nations.* ... To which is added a bibliography of English writers on angling by JOHN RUSSELL SMITH. London.

GUDGER, E. W.

1927. "Wooden Hooks Used for Catching Sharks and Ruvettus in the South Seas: A Study of Their Variation and Distribution," *Anthropological Papers of the American Museum of Natural History*, Vol. 28, Part III, pp. 197–348. New York.

LAGERCRANTZ, STURE

1934. *Fish-Hooks in Africa and Their Distribution*. Statens Etnografiska Museum—Smärre Meddelanden, Vol XII. Stockholm.

PETERS, NIKOLAUS

1935. *Angeln*. ("Handbuch der Seefischerei Nordeuropas," Tome 4, Vol. II.) Stuttgart.

PHILLIPS, W. J.

1948. "A Collection of Maori Fish Hooks," *Ethnos*, XIII, 44–53. Stockholm.

INDEX

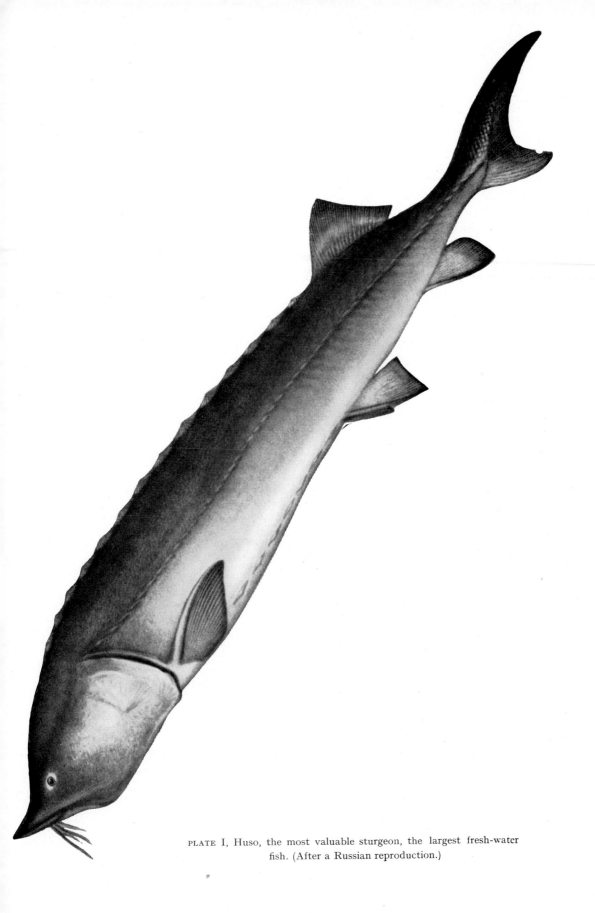

PLATE I, Huso, the most valuable sturgeon, the largest fresh-water
fish. (After a Russian reproduction.)

PLATE II, No. 1. Bronze hook for huso fishing from the early Iron Age, transitory period A–B, Hallstatt culture. Ispánlaka, Transylvania. (After Dumitrescu.)

PLATE II, No. 2. Huso fishing with anchor-shaped hook. Region of Iron Gate, Danube. (From the margin of Libay's map of the Danube, drawn in 1788.) Note floating pumpkin *(right edge of picture)* to which the hook was fastened (for constructional design see Fig. 6).

PLATE III, No. 1. Anchor-shaped huso hook. Apatin, middle Danube. (In the Budapest Ethnographical Museum.) Length, 7 cm; extreme width, 14,7 cm.

PLATE III, No. 2. Anchor-shaped chained huso hook. Apatin, middle Danube. (In the Budapest Ethnographical Museum). Length, 25 cm; extreme width, 20 cm.

PLATE IV, No. 1. Anchor-shaped chained huso hook. Apatin, middle Danube. (In the Budapest Ethnographical Museum.) Length, 23,7 cm.; extreme width, 20,5 cm.

PLATE IV, No. 2. Anchor-shaped huso hook suspended from wire. Region of Iron Gate, Danube. (In the Budapest Agricultural Museum.) Length, 17,3 cm.; extreme width, 25 cm.

PLATE V, No. 1. Serially arranged anchor-shaped huso hooks before weir (Hungarian, *cége*; Serbian, *garde*). Vrbica, south of Iron Gate, lower Danube. (After a lithograph of Alt, published in 1826.)

PLATE V, No. 2. Serially arranged anchor-shaped huso hooks before weir. Svištov, south of Iron Gate, lower Danube. (After a lithograph of Alt, published in 1826.)

PLATE VI, No. 2. Huso hook, Type II. Apatin, middle Danube. (In the Budapest Ethnographical Museum.) For constructional design see Fig. 18.

PLATE VI, No. 1. Huso hook, Type I. Danube. (In the Budapest Ethnographical Museum.) For constructional design see Fig. 16.

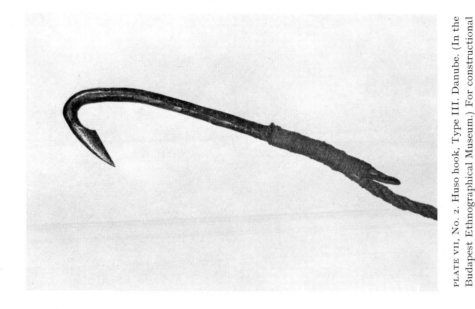

PLATE VII, No. 2. Huso hook, Type III. Danube. (In the Budapest Ethnographical Museum.) For constructional design see Fig. 20.

PLATE VII, No. 1. Huso hook, Type II, with float. Danube. (In the Budapest Ethnographical Museum.) For constructional design see Fig. 19.

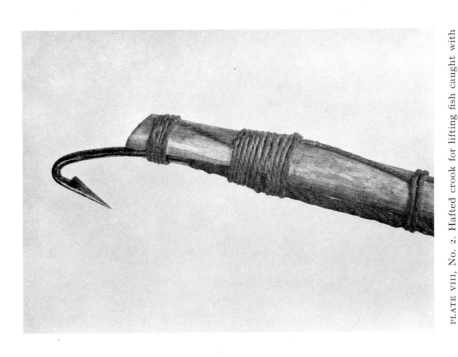

PLATE VIII, No. 2. Hafted crook for lifting fish caught with huso hook of Type IV. Apatin, middle Danube. (In the Budapest Ethnographical Museum.) For constructional design see Fig. 28.

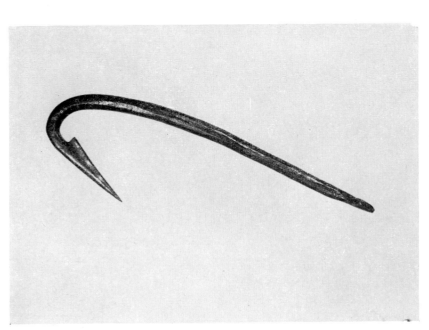

PLATE VIII, No. 1. Huso hook, Type IV. Apatin, middle Danube. (In the Budapest Ethnographical Museum.) For constructional design see Fig. 27.

PLATE IX, No. 2. Huso hook, Type V, made from industrially manufactured wire. Tolna, middle Danube. (In the Budapest Ethnographical Museum.) For constructional design see Fig. 30.

PLATE IX, No. 1. Forged huso hook of Type V. Apatin, middle Danube. (In the Budapest Ethnographical Museum.) For constructional design see Fig. 29.

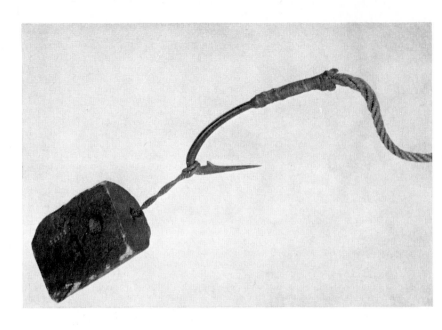

PLATE X, No. 2. Forged huso hook of Type V, with float. Danube. (In the Budapest Ethnographical Museum.) For constructional design see Fig. 32.

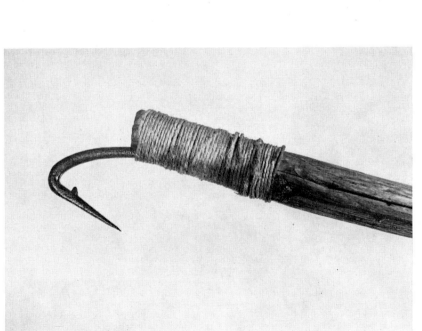

PLATE X, No. 1. Hafted crook for lifting fish caught with huso hook of Type V. Apatin, Middle Danube. (In the Budapest Ethnographical Museum.) For constructional design see Fig. 31.

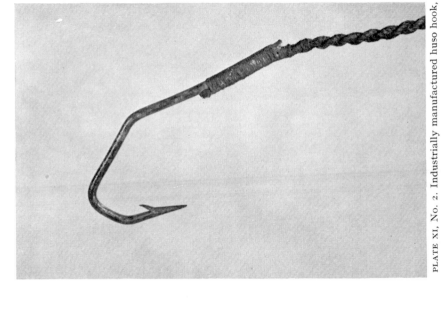

PLATE XI, No. 2. Industrially manufactured huso hook, Type VII. Apatin, middle Danube. (In the Budapest Ethnographical Museum.) For constructional design see Fig. 35.

PLATE XI, No. 1. Hanging huso hook of Type VI, made from industrially manufactured wire. Danube. (In the Budapest Ethnographical Museum.) For constructional design see Fig. 33.

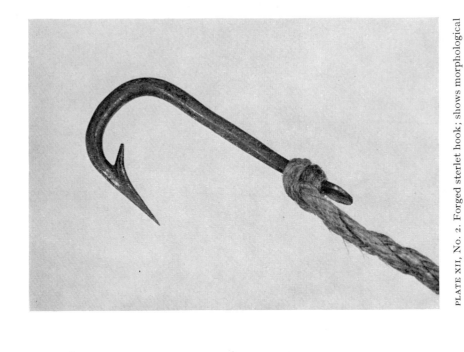

PLATE XII, No. 2. Forged sterlet hook; shows morphological traces of sheatfish hooks but is adapted to sturgeon fishing. Mohács, middle Danube. (In the Budapest Ethnographical Museum.) For constructional design see Fig. 40.

PLATE XII, No. 1. Industrially manufactured huso hook, Type VIII. Mohács, middle Danube. (In the Budapest Ethnographical Museum.) For constructional design see Fig. 36.

PLATE XIII, No. 2. Industrially manufactured sterlet hook with cork. Mohács, middle Danube. (In the Budapest Ethnographical Museum.) For constructional design see Fig. 42.

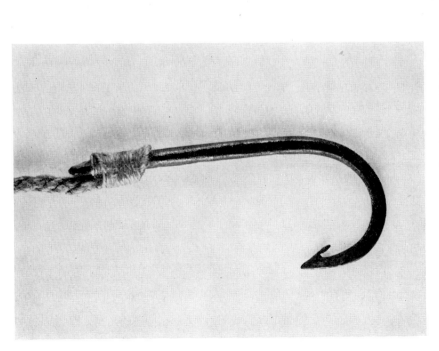

PLATE XIII, No. 1. Sheatfish hook of typical shape illustrates its similarity to sterlet hook shown in preceding plate. Tisza. (In the Musée de l'Homme, Paris.) For constructional design see Fig. 41.

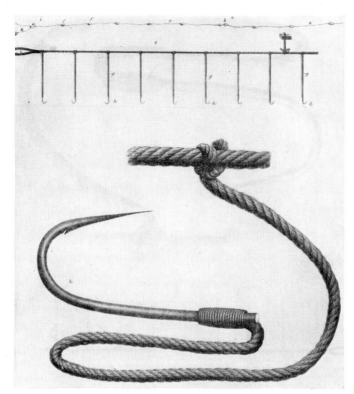

PLATE XIV, No. 1. Suspended (floatless) huso hook of the samolov type. Caspian Sea. (After Šul'c.)

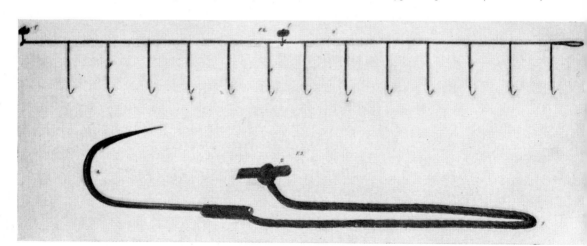

PLATE XIV, No. 2. Suspended (floatless) huso hook of the samolov type. Volga. (After Šul'c.)

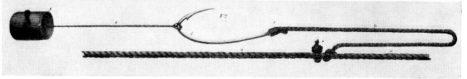

PLATE XIV, No. 3. Sterlet hook of the samolov type, which float. Dvina. (After Šul'c.)

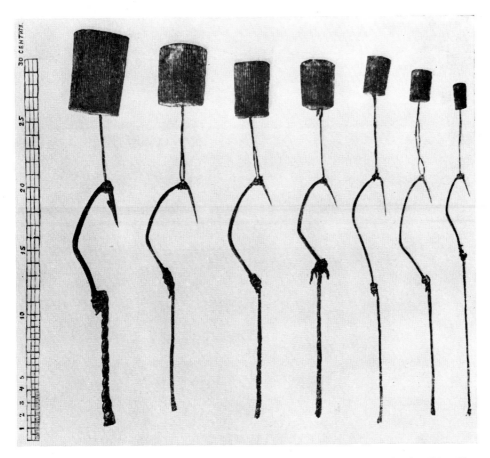

PLATE XV, Nos. 1–7. Sturgeon hooks of the samolov type. Ob Basin, West Siberia. (After Varpakhovskij.)

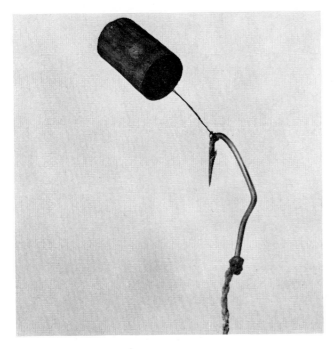

PLATE XV, No. 8. Sterlet hook
of the samolov type. Middle Ob,
West Siberia. (In the Budapest
Ethnographical Museum.) Float
made of black poplar *(Populus
nigra)*, the line of the float of
black horsehair.
Length, 10,5 cm.

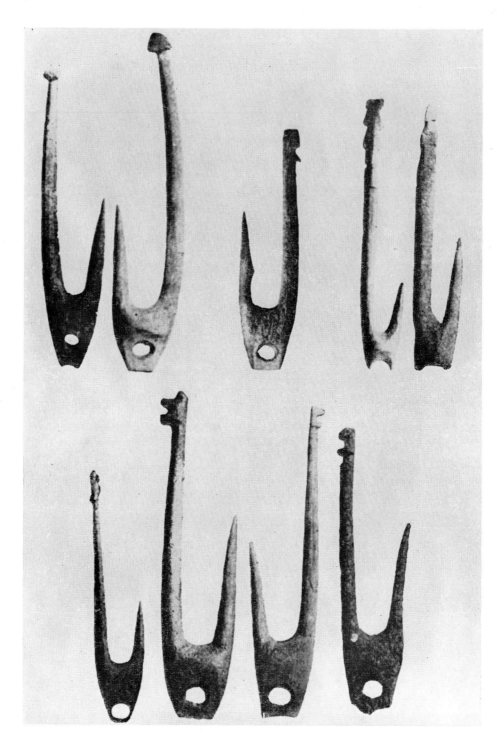

PLATE XVI, Nos. 1–9. Lappic hooks made of reindeer horn, from the Viking period. Kjelmø Island, Varanger Fiord, Norway. (After Solberg.) Lengths: 9.4 cm., 10.5 cm., 7.9 cm., 8.7 cm., 8.2 cm., 7.8 cm., 10.3 cm., 9.9 cm., and 8.9 cm.

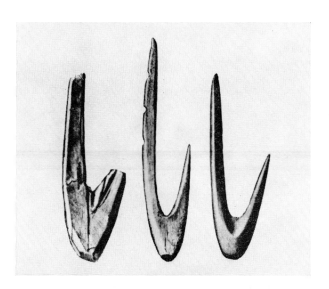

PLATE XVII, Nos. 1–3. A semifinished and two finished staghorn hooks from a mesolithic kitchen-midden find *(kjøkkenmødding)*. Viste, near Stavanger, Norway. (After Brøgger.)

PLATE XVII, No. 4. Recent bone hook. Tami Island, New Guinea. (In the Budapest Ethnographical Museum.) Length, 5.9 cm.

PLATE XVII, Nos. 5–9. Recent composite (wood and bone) hooks. Finland. (After Pälsi.)

PLATE XVIII, No. 1. Wooden hook of fishing dragon. Hook made of bamboo, the uniting bast of the fibers of *asita* nut. Baava, Popoko Island, Solomons. (In the Musée de l'Homme, Paris.) Length, 6.5cm.

PLATE XVIII, No. 2. Composite hook (stone and bone). New Hebrides, Melanesia. (In the Budapest Ethnographical Museum.) Length, 8.7 cm.

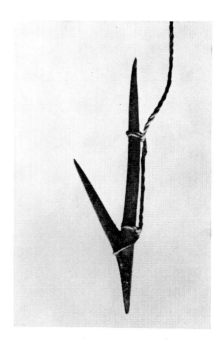

PLATE XVIII, No. 3. Composite hook (bone and horn). Used without bait for the capture of a fish called *atun*. Bougainville, Tiop Island, Solomons. (In the Musée de l'Homme, Paris.) Length, 9 cm.

PLATE XVIII, No. 4. Hook made from a single branch. Finland. (After Pälsi.)

PLATE XIX, No. 1. Iron sterlet hook of the samolov type. *Middle Ob*, West Siberia. (In the Budapest Ethnographical Museum.) Float made of black poplar *(Populus nigra)*, the line of the float of white horsehair. Length, 6 cm.

PLATE XIX, Nos. 2–10. Lappic reindeer-horn hooks from the Viking period. Kjelmø Island, Varanger Fiord, Norway. (After Solberg.) Lengths, 12.1 cm., 9.8 cm., 8.1 cm., 6.1 cm., 7.8 cm., 5.1 cm., 8.7 cm., 6 cm., and 8.5 cm.

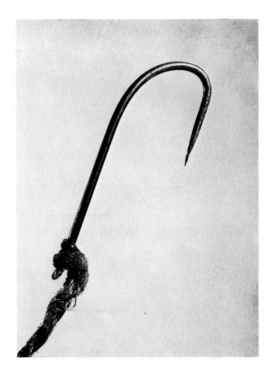

PLATE XX, No. 1. Industrially manufactured hook
of the samolov type (originally provided with float).
Amur. (In the Budapest Ethnographical Museum.)
Length, 12.4 cm.

PLATE XX, No. 2. Fossil Eskimo samolov
made of walrus tusk. Point Hope, Alaska.
(After Mathiassen.) Length, 3.6 cm.

PLATE XX, No. 3. Fossil Eskimo hook.
Shank, reindeer horn, crook, bone.
Barter Island, northeastern Alaska.
(After Mathiassen.) Length, 9 cm.

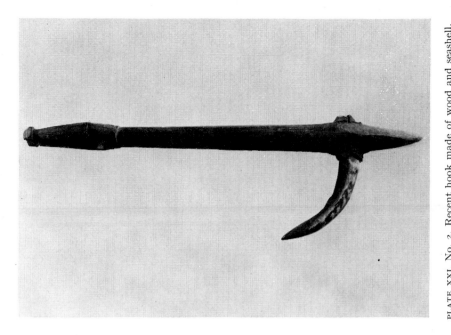

PLATE XXI, No. 2. Recent hook made of wood and seashell. Admirality Islands, New Guinea. (In the Musée de l'Homme, Paris.) Length, 28.6 cm.

PLATE XXI, No. 1. Stone hook from the Pitware culture. Anholt, Kattegat, Denmark. (After Glob.) Length, 9.2 cm.

PLATE XXII. Hammering the point of the huso hook. Lower Danube. (After Antipa.)

PLATE XXIII, No. 1. Floats for sterlet hooks of the
samolov type, tied together. Volga. (After Šul'c.)

PLATE XXIII, No. 2. Huso hooks drying on bifurcate branches. Lower Danube. (After Antipa.)

PLATE XXIII, No. 3. Hooking gear of the samolov
type hanging from bifurcate branch. Volga.
(After Šul'c.)

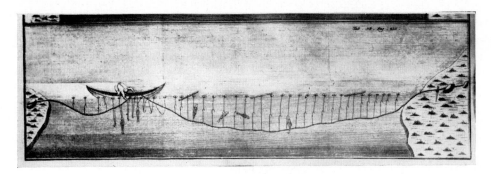

PLATE XXIV, No. 1. Row of floating huso hooks across the river, eighteenth century. Volga. (After Gmelin.)

PLATE XXIV, No. 2. Set up of floated samolov hooks across the river, nineteenth century. Volga. (After Sul'c.)

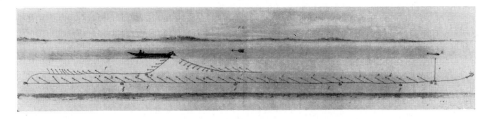

PLATE XXIV, No. 3. Set up of floated samolov hook along the current, nineteenth century. Volga. (After Šul'c.)